# Bear
# Encounters

True Stories to Entertain and Educate

North American Bear Center

Adventure Publications, Inc.
Cambridge, MN

The stories in this book were submitted by the general public to the North American Bear Center and their inclusion should not be considered an endorsement of the practices or activities described in them. Regarding the feeding of bears, Dr. Rogers makes this statement on www.bearstudy.org, "I do not recommend people feed bears even though I do it as part of my research. Feeding bears in residential areas can get bears killed because people's attitudes vary." For more information on Dr. Rogers's research, see his website, www.bearstudy.org.

Edited by Brett Ortler and Janice Edens

Photo Credits
 p. 6 by Laura Gillespie
 p. 26 by Lorraine Kalal
 p. 52 by Laura Gillespie
 p. 90 by Elizabeth Rogers Tiller, PhD
 p. 122 by Susan Moore
 front cover by Jackie Orsulak
 back cover by Susan Moore

Book and cover design by Jonathan Norberg

10 9 8 7 6 5 4 3 2 1
Copyright 2013 by North American Bear Center
Published by Adventure Publications, Inc.
820 Cleveland Street South
Cambridge, MN 55008
1-800-678-7006
www.adventurepublications.net
All rights reserved
ISBN: 978-1-59193-384-7

# Table of Contents

**BEARS HAVE BEEN MISUNDERSTOOD** for most of modern history. The violent killers portrayed in movies and hunting magazines bear no resemblance to the timid animals researchers study in the wild. Instead of being aggressive, meat-obsessed carnivores, these omnivores typically seek the safety of solitude and a diet of nuts, leaves, berries and insects. In short, much of what is popularly "known" about black bears is a myth.

Dr. Lynn Rogers founded the North American Bear Center to replace those myths with facts. The Center's research produces scientific knowledge that has practical applications for residents of bear country. The biggest benefit of knowing the truth about black bears is that it helps people enjoy bear country without unnecessary fear.

Nowhere is this clearer than in the accounts of actual bear encounters. In 2010, the North American Bear Center invited its fans to submit their own bear encounter stories. This book is the result. Organized by the myths they debunk, these stories are literal proof that black bears are not the threat they are perceived to be. Many of the accounts are testaments to this. Many people who were fearful during their encounters viewed bears differently after visiting the North American Bear Center or learning of Lynn Rogers's work. The "threatening" behavior that some of the bears seemed to exhibit turned out to be an expression of the bears' own nervousness, not a sign of aggression. That's the North American Bear Center's primary goal—to help the public see bears for what they really are, animals we can understand, respect and admire, not animals we should blindly fear.

*Submitted online by fans of the North American Bear Center, the stories in this book stem from real-life observations of bears. From bear encounters in yards, on porches and driveways, to more up-close-and-personal interactions, these stories will give you a glimpse of what wild bears are really like.*

# Not Exactly Vicious

# FICTION:

## Black bears are violent killers.

# FACT:

## Black bears are anything but violent.

Black bears look like predators, but they don't act like it. They almost always flee from people. (That's why many of the stories in this section are brief encounters that consist of bears running away.) Where black bears are used to seeing people, they tend to ignore them. Only one black bear in a million actually kills someone. Truth be told, they behave more like prey animals. That's because not long ago, during the ice ages, they were prey, falling victim to dire wolves, saber-tooth cats, and giant short-faced bears. These powerful predators, now extinct, couldn't climb trees and black bears survived by being wary and ready to climb. That timid attitude is still apparent today. That's why black bears are occasionally "treed" by such "predators" as housecats and the family dog.

This collection of stories demonstrates that the black bear's natural tendency after encountering humans is to simply move on.

# The Most Aggressive Bear I Ever Met

THE MOST AGGRESSIVE BEAR I ever met may also have been the hungriest. An old wound had withered her right front leg. She limped on three legs, eating berries and greens but nothing that required climbing, digging or turning over rocks. She was famished when I met her in 1984. Berries were scarce, and she was trying to make milk for three cubs.

She became notorious when she entered a house and scared 74-year-old Toini Salminen. Toini had lost her husband to a logging accident a few years earlier and was living alone in a remote cabin beside Little Long Lake outside Ely, Minnesota. Just after dark, Toini went on instant alert when someone or something opened her door and began rummaging in her entryway. When she heard a bag of dog food being dragged out the door, she knew what it was. The sounds faded. Toini waited. Then she cautiously went to the open door and locked it—something the trusting folks of her area seldom did.

Toini lay awake that night. What if the bear came again? She stopped walking the quarter mile to her mailbox each day. She checked outside her windows every time she went out.

She called me. I'd heard of her. On the phone, I discovered she had a delightful manner and a Finnish accent. She described what happened. When I mentioned what people usually do when bears enter their houses, she told me how her husband had loved wildlife and wouldn't have wanted the bear killed or moved away from its cubs. I suggested the only other option that came to mind, "If you put food outside, the bear won't need to come in."

She paused and said, "I think my husband would like that."

I responded, "Okay, I'll bring a bag of beef fat from Zup's store." I had no idea what I was about to run into.

I drove up, carried the bag of fat to her door, and knocked. Before she could come, the bear came out of the woods limping straight for the bag in my arms. I kicked at her, but she agilely dodged and darted in almost faster than I could kick again. I kicked and kicked until the door opened and I could dart inside.

I was shaken and out of breath. The bear and I had not touched each other, but the encounter reminded me too much of ferocious images I'd seen in hunting magazines. I said, "That bear should be shot! It could hurt someone! I've never seen a bear like that!"

"No, we feed her!" she said decisively.

That began Toini's twelve-year relationship with the bear she named Gloria. After she gave the bag of fat to Gloria, Toini placed pans of dog food outside her kitchen window. Each day, she looked forward to the clank of the lid and seeing Gloria and her cubs lie down in a circle to share Toini's offering.

Toini began to see the bears in a new light. She ventured outside, not sure how they would react. They retreated! Toini often went outside with them after that but kept her distance. The bears began to trust her. Toini resumed her daily walks to the mailbox. Friends and neighbors (including my family and I) came to see the bears. They kept their distance, too. Soon the bears paid little attention to people in the safety of Toini's yard. Toini took things further. When no one was around, she tossed treats to Gloria, drawing her closer and closer until Gloria would gently take them from her hand.

Toini also gave treats to my wife and girls. A Pepsi was always waiting in the refrigerator for me. We loved Toini. We all spent time together, and

Gloria was part of it.

A special memory came in late July 1988. We all had sat down at a picnic table where Toini had brought out hot dogs, potato salad, warm cookies, and carrot cake. We were putting together hot dogs when Toini looked up and said, "Hi *Gloooria*," in her familiar voice. Gloria was newly back after being gone for 10 months. Where Gloria lived for 10–11 months each year was a mystery, but when she returned, she was immediately comfortable with people in Toini's yard. She limped confidently to the table. Colleen (7) turned to look, but Kelly (8) continued putting catsup on her hot dog. She'd seen plenty of bears, including Gloria, and didn't care that Gloria was three feet behind her. Toini tossed a cookie. Gloria ate it, then eased in beside Colleen to steal a package of hot dog buns. We kept eating. Gloria did the same on the ground with the buns. When she was done, she sat well-mannered beside the table. What a change from the hungry, aggressive bear I'd met four years earlier.

Toini and Gloria went on for another eight years. As far as we know, Gloria never approached anyone outside Toini's yard and never touched anyone except to gently accept food from Toini's hand.

Each year, Gloria stopped visiting Toini in September, bear-hunting season, leaving Toini to worry about Gloria's survival until Gloria showed up the next July or August.

Toini was getting older. People urged her to move into town. But seeing Gloria was what made her world right. She and Gloria each recognized a side in the other that most people and bears don't realize exists in the other.

Bad news came in September 1996. A bear-hunter eight miles away killed an unusually old female with worn teeth and a withered right front leg. Toini, 86, moved into town that winter but returned two more summers in case Gloria showed up. For the rest of her years, this delightful lady and her many friends continued to remember how Gloria had drawn them together and enriched their lives.

**LYNN ROGERS** ELY, MN

# Get Outta Here!

MY STORY TAKES PLACE back in the 1960s. My mom, dad, brother and I went to visit old friends in Wisconsin. We camped in the Chequamegon-Nicolet National Forest. Mom, Dad and I had a smaller tent; my brother had his own tent to sleep in. My mom and dad had cots to sleep on, and I slept in the center, between them, in a sleeping bag on an air mattress.

Needless to say, Mom never really slept the best. She said she could always hear the animals outside, like the bears going after the garbage cans. They made an awful racket. She said she could even hear critters run across the tent at night, and she knew there were skunks out there, too, because the night we set up our tents (we got there late), we had to do it by flashlights and the skunks were always walking by, checking us out.

One night my dad had brought some oranges and/or bananas in the tent, not thinking, I guess, and in the middle of the night my mom hollered, "VIRG!" (my dad's name). Out of a deep sleep, he awoke and saw a bear sticking his nose and paw into our tent. He slapped the bear and yelled, "GET OUTTA HERE!" The poor bear turned and *ran*.

**CAROL BARTELS** SAUK RAPIDS, MN

# The Twin Lakes Bear

IN 1968 OR 1969, when I was about nine or ten years old, my family and I were camping in a little ten-site campground called Twin Lakes near Lac du Flambeau, Wisconsin. There was a bear trap in the area (for relocation), but we had never seen a bear there.

One afternoon, after our dad and a fellow camper had gone fishing the night before and caught a bunch of rainbow trout, our parents sent us down to the other end of the campground to invite the other family for supper that evening to enjoy a fish fry. The campsites were all located along one side of the lake, with woods on the other side of the road. We had almost arrived at their campsite, when right in front of us five kids, a bear started to come out of the woods, probably intending to cross the road. Some of us screamed, but we *all* ran—my sister and I back down the road towards our site, and two of my brothers down the trail next to the lake. My youngest brother (who was around three years old at the time) took off cross-country, running through everyone's campsites, even falling down once, but getting up so fast that before the people sitting around the campfire could even help pick him up, he was off and running again! We were almost too scared to notice that the poor bear was so afraid it took off running in the other direction!

When we got back to camp (I think I was the fastest runner!), my parents scolded me. Since I was the oldest, I should have made certain that the younger kids were okay. I insisted it was everyone for himself if a bear was chasing us (which it wasn't), but we were just dumb little kids at the time. We all got scolded because our parents told us the bear wasn't going to hurt us, and it was probably more afraid of us than we were of it (I highly doubt it—we were pretty scared at the time) and that there was no need to create such a ruckus, for goodness sake!

In retellings of this story, facts would sometimes become a little embroidered—my youngest brother ran through a flaming campfire, or the bear growled at us before he ran the other way, or the bear stood up on his hind legs and growled at us before running the other way, or even the bear chased us for a while before running the other way! I can assure you that none of this happened, and the true story is the one given above. Poor bear—he probably begged to be relocated after coming in contact with the likes of us!

**KATHY BRUNER** WISCONSIN RAPIDS, WI

# Bear in the Butter

MANY POINT IS A BOY SCOUT CAMP situated near the headwaters of the Mississippi River. Located on 2400 acres, it surrounds Many Point Lake in northwestern Minnesota. It is home to over 200 troops from numerous councils across the United States and Canada. The summer of 1997 at Many Point, my son, Rick (then fifteen years old), was camping for a week with scouts from his troop. One late morning, he and a fellow scout were in their four-person tent, which had entrances at both ends, reading books. They heard a ruckus outside, looked out and saw an adult black bear trying to get at their cooler that contained butter. They were curious but knew to stay put and ignore the bear, having heard tales of black bear encounters. So they stayed quiet in the tent.

The cooler was hanging in a tree, which is the normal practice for keeping food away from bears. The bear was relentless. It got the cooler (a metal one) down and tore it open with its claws and teeth. After devouring the butter, it ventured to the tent where the scouts were quietly (and fearfully!) huddled in their beds. The bear entered the tent and proceeded out the other end, oblivious to the scouts' presence. They never saw the bear again.

This bear was the resident thief at Many Point and had a police record. It had been trapped at least three times and moved a hundred or more miles away but always returned for the easy pickings. When the camp was devoid of scouts, many weekends were spent tracking and trapping the bear.

This bear appeared to be no threat to scouts, having passed so close to them. The scouts were informed of bear activity and that keeping food on themselves was not permitted. Abiding by the rules and common sense made them just another object in the bear's habitat.

**NANCY STANZ** KIMBALL, MN

# Stumbling on Bears

**WHEN MY HUSBAND WAS YOUNGER** (he thinks five or six) his brother (eight or nine years old) was riding his bicycle and rode into Brownie, a bear that frequented Vince Shute's place. He flew over the bicycle handles and the bear, but the bear just looked at him and walked away.

When I was a child, we went out to Vince Shute's a lot; my grandparents were friends of his. We recall bears everywhere, but no incidents. My cousin once stooped down and reached out for one of the bear cubs. The cub was curious, but wary, and slowly walked up to her hand to sniff it. Mama and siblings were watching from the nearby tree. From what I can remember, it touched my cousin's hand with its nose and then ran up the tree. It was adorable!

ERICKA IVERSON ORR, MN

# Close Encounters of the Bruin Kind

WE WERE A MIXED GROUP OF EIGHT, ages 13–40, backpacking an eighty-mile mid-July trek in King's Canyon in the Sierra Nevada Mountains in California in 1984. The rangers gave us ample warning of the bears in the area, specifically that bears had figured out how to untie the knots in the cable ties used to hang the food packs at each campsite. Indeed, we had bears visit our camp every night along the way. They were unsuccessful at obtaining the food pack, but successful at puncturing several of our plastic water containers. The most significant encounter occurred the last evening of our hike. Since it was an eight-day hike at higher elevations, we'd carefully planned and packed just enough food for the journey, and this was to be our last full meal. As we approached the campsite, we noted a sow and her two cubs nearby. We crossed the stream on a downed log and proceeded to set up camp and prepare dinner. Back on the other side of the stream, the sow treed her two cubs and crossed the stream to our side, circumventing the cooking area and positioning herself with us between her and the treed cubs. We knew this was not a place we

**15**

wanted to be, between a mother bear and her cubs. But we were not about to give up our remaining food after the day's long trek, either. So we armed ourselves with the tin plates and utensils from the mess kit, along with the giant pine cones scattered on the ground, and we assumed position. After several moments, the sow charged twelve feet toward us, then abruptly stopped. It happened so quickly that none of us reacted! Realizing it was our turn to take action, we started to make a scene—yelling, banging the tin plates and tossing the pine cones. The sow immediately gave it up, circled the camp and proceeded back across the stream to the treed cubs. We kept a wary eye on her and began eating our last dinner in the Sierras. Summoning her cubs from the tree, she brought them to our side of the stream. Luckily, they made no effort to bother us or attempt to take our food, but they did mill around the area. The two cubs tussled and sparred with each other, showing us the white patches on their chests, providing us with entertainment and laughter during dinner. A delightful finale to the wonderfully rugged hike!

**LAURIE ATHMANN** DULUTH, MN

# A Bear Visits the Town

LAST SUMMER, there were many reports of sightings of a small black bear in our small semi-rural town. It had even made a visit to our local town hall, which is surrounded by a lake and woods. I happened to go there to pick up some trash bags for our town clean-up day, scheduled for the following weekend. While at the town hall, everyone was talking about the bear in town. You would have thought we were being invaded by aliens! One man present had photos on his cell phone of the bear eating garbage from the unsecured trash cans at town hall. The photo was obviously taken within a few feet of this bear. I looked at the photos and realized this was a small sub-adult black bear, very likely just passing through after the family break-up. All the people present were "scared of the bear" and were talking about what they would do if they saw it. You see, the local media was trying to make this bear out to be some kind of "threat to the community." This saddened me, as it was apparent the bear was a young male, just passing through in search of his new territory and life alone. He was trying to figure out how to find natural food sources and survive on his own for the first time in his young life. I asked if the bear did anything that was threatening or in any way showed he was not afraid of people. The group explained that every time anyone would get near the bear, he would "clack his jaws," run away and climb the nearest tree. I explained this is exactly what a bear should do. This behavior meant the bear still had a natural fear of humans, was nervous when approached, and did not pose a threat, as the media had tried to report. I tried my best to explain that the bear was just passing through the area as many bears do without ever being seen. The group was surprised to hear that this area is a natural corridor for bears due to the large state park that borders our town and the vast Catskill Mountains further north. I was very pleased to convince the group that they needed to secure the trash cans at town hall and the adjacent volunteer fire department, so not only a bear, but also other wild animals, could not get into the trash. I hope I was able to convince the group that the bear was not the threat the local media was portraying it to be. Nothing I was told even remotely indicated that this bear was a threat or aggressive in any way. It is interesting to note that the area was in a severe drought during the time of the bear's visit. I suspect the bear just happened upon an easy food source, while making its way out of its mother's territory and while seeking its own new territory.

**CYNTHIA WULKAN-FONTANE** PUTNAM VALLEY, NY

# Hoping to Conquer Fear

**YEARS AGO A GIRLFRIEND OF MINE** went up to the Vince Shute Sanctuary to see the bears. These were the days that when you parked your car and got out, you were right there among the bears. I decided to do this to try to conquer my fear—well, I tell you, the hair on my arms stood so high you could practically braid it! To this day, I still have the fear, due to very scary dreams when I was a kid. I love Lily and Hope to death, though, and maybe one day my fear of bears will pass.

**VIV MUELLER** AURORA, MN

# Bears Just Want to Have Dinner

A FRIEND AND I HAD A FINE DINNER one night in Green Mountain Falls, Colorado, (near Colorado Springs) while on vacation. After dinner, we took a walk around the pond near the center of town. At one point we noticed dogs barking hysterically and looked up to see a small black bear ambling down the street. To my friend's dismay, I followed the bear as it wandered down into town. It walked alongside the buildings, stopping to nibble some berries off a bush. I got as close as I felt comfortable and snapped a photo. The bear seemed far less interested in me than in the berries. It moved farther down the street until a group of people gathered to watch it. The bear was now cornered between people and buildings and, appearing to be frightened, it ran off into the woods behind the town square.

We continued our walk around the town and when we arrived on the other side of the square, we discovered the bear sitting atop a garbage bin. I again got too close for my friend's comfort to take another photo of the bear who continued to ignore me in favor of food. The garbage bin was situated near the office of the sheriff, who happened out, saw the bear, retrieved a pellet gun and, assuring us that he would not hurt the bear, sent it on its way with one shot. He pointed out that this would keep the bear from venturing into the garbage again and then told me just how unwise I had been to get so close to such a dangerous creature. I heard him, but I didn't really believe him. This bear didn't seem too dangerous to me. Hungry, yes. Dangerous, no.

Having been educated by Dr. Rogers, I now know I was likely correct in my estimation of the situation.

LORRAINE POTTER KALAL KNOXVILLE, TN

# Just Passing Through

ONE DAY MY HUSBAND was washing his car in our driveway as he often does. While he was doing that, our neighbor Enrique across the street saw a bear walking in his back yard. Enrique grabbed his camera and went outside to get a picture of the bear. When he went outside, the bear was leaving his front yard and crossing the street to head up our driveway, where my husband was busily washing the bottom of his car. My husband looked up a little and saw Enrique taking pictures of him washing his car. It puzzled Peter, so he got up when he finished the side and went across the street to ask Enrique. Enrique told him that the biggest bear he had ever seen had just walked up our driveway and walked just past the other side of the car that Peter was washing. We have a fish and game reserve behind our backyard, and that is where the bear was heading. If Peter hadn't seen Enrique taking pictures, he would have never known that the bear had come so close and just passed him by.

**JOAN TENEWITZ** MORRIS COUNTY, NJ

# Bears? What Bears?
# Four Bears?

CONSIDERING THE SIGNS of bear activity that I have seen while mowing and hiking on our family farm in Bedford County, Virginia, I've had surprisingly few encounters with bears. My first bear encounter was more of a near-miss. It occurred on a beautiful day in August 2008 when I was painting siding on my small house. The first part of the day, I painted on the southeast side, but when the sun became too high and hot, I retreated to the northwest side. While on the ladder on the shaded side, I heard a ruckus in the woods behind me. At the time, I attributed it to the fact that squirrels can make a lot of noise. I didn't even bother to look and just kept on painting. So, later in the day, as the sun was lower in the sky, I took my ladder and materials back over to the southeast side to finish up the job. While there, a neighbor who lives farther up the quiet gravel road drove by and stopped his truck and called out to get my attention. After I realized he was calling for me, I climbed down the ladder, waved and called out, "What's up?" He then asked me if I had seen the mother bear and her three cubs that had been relaxing earlier in the day in another part of the yard, just out of sight, over a small knoll. This is an area that they apparently loved because it has large pine trees and several fruit trees, including their favorite, an old pear tree. He let me know that they were there with regularity, and other neighbors had also seen them. Needless to say, I really wished I had seen them, but was grateful that I didn't notice them while I was perched on the ladder! The next time I hear a ruckus in the woods, I think I'll take a look.

MONICA L. MARTIN CHRISTIANSBURG, VA

# Visits with Little Bear

TODAY I HAD THE MOST incredible experience of my life. It all began about 5:45 a.m. I saw Vinnie, my cat, sitting on the bench by the peach tree staring intently into the bushes—as it turns out, he was staring at a little baby bear. I went to close up shop, and when I got back, there was a big ginger-colored bear and the baby bear was gone. I chased away the big bear and waited around for the baby bear to come back. Soon baby bear returned, sat down a bit and then started to walk down to the creek. Suddenly it snorted, got very nervous and ran up the embankment. I looked and saw the big old ginger bear lurking and again I chased it away. From then on I was baby bear's hero. I was incredulous when the bear walked down to the edge of the water and sat on the rock with Vinnie. I snagged some photos. Pretty soon the bear went on the grass and sat down, reclining on its back, scratching his belly with his front paw. It's amazing how human they can look.

On another occasion, I went down to the creek with Vinnie, and Molly, another one of my cats. We sat for about 15 minutes when I saw their ears perk up and they began staring down at the creek. It wasn't long before Little Bear appeared. Vinnie started a little face-off, cat-growling at the bear and starting to cross the creek. Little Bear got real nervous—snorting and prancing around. I got up and told Vinnie to leave that bear alone. Little Bear ran up the hill a ways. I sat on the other side of the creek and as it began to get dark, Little Bear walked away up the hill.

**MARIE BRAVO** MARKLEEVILLE, CA

# "Grandma, There's a Bear Out There!"

I **LIVE IN A CONGESTED AREA** on Cross Lake outside of Pine City, MN. This past summer I had a bear visit my property. My seven-year-old granddaughter Lyric called to me, "Grandma, there's a bear out there." I said, "Oh no, Lyric, it must be the neighbor's dog." She insisted, saying, "No, Grandma, it's a bear!" So I went to the sliding glass door and there was a bear! A great big black bear! It was frolicking along our lakeshore and slapping the water. It looked like the bear was having fun. The next moment the bear leapt upon my dock and then dived into the water. We were so excited as the bear came up and was swimming along. I was amazed how far out of the water it was carrying itself with ease. It was a day we will always remember.

**JANE LEVERENZ** PINE CITY, MN

# Welcome Home

**EDITOR'S NOTE:** Years ago, Stewart and Kathy Hornby befriended a wild male black bear (which they named Bruno) at their Wildernest Inn in the mountains of West Virginia. Each year they watch for his return after hibernation. Kathy sent this email to a friend in March 2008:

Our beloved Bruno returned this week. GREAT excitement and needless to say buckets of tears from me! He is now eight years old. This is the longest he has ever denned—early October to late February. He is the first bear to make an appearance this year. Our Jack Russell (Scud) went crazy when Bruno appeared at our bedroom door. He was licking Bruno's face and Scud's little tail was going full speed. Even the cat ran up to greet the big boy, who is over 450 pounds.

**EDITOR'S NOTE:** In 2010, Bruno was late showing up. Stewart and Kathy thought he was dead. Kathy sent this email on March 16, 2010.

Well, it was obviously the "right" thing to do . . . Cry all night and all day . . . think the worst. But Bruno, as always, got my "vibe." BRUNO IS ALIVE! We found him on the mountain after Ugly Bear chased him off. They had a huge fight . . . Ugly had Bruno on his back. Stewart broke up the fight and sat with Bruno a while. How does this happen? Bruno has been the King of the Mountain for years. I cannot tell you how relieved I am; I hope he somehow makes his way to Mama. I cannot wait for my kisses. My prayers have been answered.

**STEWART AND KATHY HORNBY** WILDERNEST INN, ROUGH RUN, WV

# I Don't Think That's a Rock

**MY ENCOUNTER BEGINS** with a trip to Idyllwild, California, for a weekend of fun in the mountains with my best friend of 36 years. We were staying in a cabin in Pine Cove and asked the owner where we could find some of the huge pine cones for which the area is famous. He suggested we hike up to the radio tower. We ended up driving up and, equipped with our bags, we started down the rocky peninsula gathering them as we went. I was particularly worried about coming up on snakes, so I was talking loudly and shuffling my feet. We got a few hundred feet apart from each other. I noticed a rock that was an unusual color of brown, and sort of reddish. The others that were rounded were more black. I thought, "Maybe it is a dead animal" and looked up into the sky for buzzards. There were none. I then called to my friend and said, "What do you think that is?" She answered, "BBBBBB, BEAR!" and started to run back up the hill. I followed, but could just hear that bear crashing through the forest after us. Of course, it didn't. It continued to enjoy its nap in the sun and wasn't even disturbed by us. When we returned to the cabin, we told the owner and he said, "Oh, yeah, we have about five black bears that we see regularly. They won't hurt you." As it turned out, that was my last big adventure with my friend, as she died from cancer soon thereafter. I will never forget our bear adventure and I have loved bears ever since.

**JEAN PARSONS** HEMET, CA

# Pass the Plants

## FICTION:

**Black bears primarily eat meat.**

## FACT:

**Black bears primarily eat plants.**

Meat is not a black bear's favorite food. Black bears have evolved as omnivores, not carnivores. Their bodies are bulky and they lack the agility to catch most animals. Bears have the long canine teeth of carnivores, but black bears primarily use these teeth to bite into logs to access ant colonies. Unlike a carnivore's teeth, a bear's cheek teeth are not scissor-like. Instead, bears have flat teeth that they use to crush food. Other omnivores, including humans and pigs, have similarly flat teeth.

Black bears do occasionally eat eggs and newborn fawns and, when preferred foods are scarce, they will eat carrion. In areas with spawning salmon, bears will eat salmon, but in most areas black bears don't eat fish. Their preferred diet is nuts, berries, vegetation and insects—especially ant pupae.

# The Pizza Story

I'VE LIVED IN THE POCONO MOUNTAINS of northeast-
ern Pennsylvania for almost 40 years and I am no stranger to bears and
their habits. My house is in a development that has state game land border-
ing it on all sides so we have a lot of wildlife around, including bears. I'm
always careful to bring in my bird feeders at night, but I still get regular
visits from my bears because others don't always bring in feeders, or they
leave food outside. We don't have a lot of neighbors, maybe 200 houses,
with about half of the residences occupied year-round, which is how I like
it. Occasionally there is a renter who has a dog, and they do not follow the
strict leash laws and leave their dog(s) loose.

A couple of summers ago there was a renter who did just that with a
large shepherd dog, and every night the dog would roam the development.
It was a friendly dog but was always getting into things around the yards
and scaring off many of the deer. One night I came home late, about 11:00
p.m., from having dinner with some friends, and I had a small box with
leftover pizza in the car.

I pulled into the driveway, and because we have no streetlights of any
kind, I'm always careful to look for critters like skunks, bears, deer, porcupines and so on. This night I was tired and apparently did not look that
carefully before I turned off the car and its headlights and opened the
driver's door. I had my left leg out the door and was reaching to the pas-
senger side to grab the pizza box and my purse when I felt the dog come up
and push into my leg with his nose.

Without really looking, I reached over with my left hand and pushed
the dog gently away by his face, still trying to get the pizza and my purse
together with my right hand. It struck me very suddenly that the dog's fur

felt very different than it should have felt, and I turned to look again as the dog came back. Its face was wedged between me and the steering wheel, and it was obviously stretching to smell the pizza.

This is when it dawned on me that the so-called dog that I'd pushed away—by his face—was a yearling black bear who was now part way inside my car, across my lap and apparently very interested in the pizza.

I happily granted his wish, and he took the box, very gently, right out of my hand, pulling it across my chest and lap. Then he walked away several feet into the woods, with some "whoof" sounds that made me think he was very happy with his prize.

I grabbed my purse and got out of the car and quietly and carefully went up the walkway and into the house. Needless to say, there was no leftover pizza for me that night!

Despite the bear's proximity, it was clear he was not interested in hurting me, and I stayed calm and quiet. In fact, he was very gentle and not threatening at all, even when I had reached out and pushed his face away from food that he was interested in. Had he wanted to, he could have hurt me very easily.

The next morning I found the pizza box about 30 feet away from the house. That's apparently the bears' favorite spot, because anything they happen to take during the night (from forgotten bird feeders to towels hung out to dry) they leave in that spot. (Apparently they like to play and drag the large bath towels around.) After watching Honey at the North American Bear Center with the stuffed bear toys this year, I will leave out a stuffed bear for my bears to see if any of them take the toy to their spot.

**KAREN** GOULDSBORO, PA

# My Honeymoon in the Dumps

**MARRIED TO LYNN HAS BEEN**... well... here's an example. For our honeymoon in 1979, instead of taking me to a fancy resort, he took me to dumps—literally. We hit vacation spots like Michigan's Copper Harbor dump, the Grand Marais dump, and others. I knew I was marrying a bear researcher, so this was not entirely unexpected.

As is usual with Lynn, we did things nobody else does, especially on a honeymoon. Most people avoid bears. We looked for them. In forests around dumps, we followed bear trails instead of hiking trails.

Things became even stranger at night. Instead of lying on a king-sized bed, we lay on bear trails, straining to distinguish bears from shadows. We learned how quietly bears walk. On well-trodden trails, breathing was their loudest sound. Bears of all sizes came very close before the two lumps in the trail flashed their cameras.

What memories! We pushed our luck and saw only timid, non-threatening behavior. I don't know how we could have made the honeymoon better. We came home wanting to know more about how these animals live. We began to wonder if researchers could walk with black bears like Lynn was doing with deer at that time.

Pictures from our honeymoon hold some of our warmest memories.

**DONNA ROGERS** ELY, MN

# Happy Hour?

SEVERAL YEARS AGO my husband was sipping a glass of wine on our deck, which overlooks Eagles Nest Lake Two. He set his wine glass down on the deck railing (about two feet high) and went into the house to check on his cooking in the kitchen. When he was about to go back out, he saw through the window that a bear cub had climbed up the nearby tree and onto the deck. The cub had placed both paws on the rail on either side of the glass and was lapping up the wine. He finished the glass without spilling a drop and lowered himself down off the deck. He joined his brother and their mother and all three wandered off. We wondered if he would return each evening around 5:00 p.m. for the cocktail hour.

CYNTHIA STOKES EAGLES NEST, MN

# Bird Feeder Snack Attack

IT WAS LATE MAY and we were sitting with our significant others in the hot tub on the deck of Susan and Pat's house near Great Smoky Mountains National Park. There were three of us in the tub; Susan had not yet joined us. The deck was narrow and the house backed up to some very dense woods. We were enjoying the serene surroundings when Pat remarked that he thought he heard a noise in the woods nearby. "It's probably a squirrel or a chipmunk," Sarah said. But the stirring in the brush continued and became louder. Upon a closer look, we could see small trees bending and shaking and hear leaves crackling, with the sound getting closer and closer to the deck. As we curiously watched this mysterious drama unfold, suddenly a small black bear stepped through an opening in the trees. The bear never looked in our direction but, instead, headed straight for the very full bird feeders which were hung immediately off the deck, less than ten feet from the hot tub. By this time we were standing up whisper-shouting things like "OMG!!! It's a bear!" and "Tell Susan to get the camera!"

As we stood or sat in the hot tub, not really knowing what to do, a second small black bear arrived and began to shake the second bird feeder pole and rise on its legs in order to swat the feeder and shake out the seed. At this point, Sarah vaulted from the hot tub, partly in fear, and partly to get her sister and her camera. (She had never vaulted before and has not since. Recovery went slowly.) Pat was barking directions to put the dogs up. All Sarah could say was "BEAR! BEAR!"

We watched the two small bears in delight. (We now realize they were yearlings, thanks to education from Lynn Rogers and the Lily Facebook fan page.) To our amazement, two even smaller bears ambled up and began to climb small trees and the bird feeder poles. They were too short to reach the feeders even on their hind legs, but had no problem shimmying up the trees. By now, all the humans were out of the hot tub and trying to figure out how these four bears were related—was it two mothers and cubs? Were they male and female siblings, with the male obviously bigger? We had no idea, when suddenly, silently and almost unnoticed, an enormous black bear emerged from the woods. She paid no attention to the four humans wildly clicking their cameras. She attempted to feed at one of the bird feeders, but a cub, who also wanted that feeder, bellowed loudly and swatted at her. She got the message and contented herself with feeding from scraps on the ground. To extract the seeds, the cubs tipped over some of the bird feeders but pulled others apart until all the seed was gone. This scene went on for several minutes. All of us had time to grab a camera and shoot multiple shots. The drama came to a close when Susan and Pat's bulldog, Leo, who had been distracted with a bowl of food, finished his treat and came out on the deck to see what was going on. He reacted to the bears with intense barking, naturally wanting to protect his humans. The bears casually acknowledged his presence. Leo's fierce barking was greeted with an almost insulting nonchalance by the bears. Mama bear simply grunted to her brood and they slowly lumbered off into the woods.

**SARAH NAYLOR CHERRY AND SUSAN NAYLOR MOORE** FRANKLIN, TN

# Build a Feeder and They Will Come

**LIVING IN OUR RURAL** Punxsutawney, Pennsylvania, home for over 40 years, we are used to hearing about and seeing our town's famous groundhog Phil, who lives year-round in his comfortable home inside the local library. On the other hand, we had only heard of bear sightings in our area but hadn't experienced any of our own until we erected a bird feeder several years ago.

My husband fashioned the feeder out of PVC pipe, with a platform on top that supported a house-like feeding station. It stood over ten feet tall in the middle of our flower garden. The birds loved it.

Much to our surprise one morning, the pipe was broken in half and the little house and seed were gone. We knew the birds weren't that strong, so we suspected a black bear. We switched to a feeder that hung from a tree branch and figured we had outsmarted our new visitor. Around 11:00 p.m. one night, we heard a noise and ventured onto our screened-in porch. There he was, climbing the tree towards his dinner. The sound of our voices brought him to the ground, and away he scampered. He probably knew he could return when we were asleep, which he did, and we found an empty feeder on the ground.

Months passed, and assuming Mr. Bear was finding his meals at our neighbor's feeders that were much more accessible, we took a chance and placed another feeder on a wire that was suspended from our gutter and was visible from our living room window. After a few weeks, a loud bang on the window interrupted our sleep at 3:00 a.m. As we turned on a spotlight, you-know-who was sitting by the house, holding the feeder, and pouring breakfast into his mouth. Just for sheer fun and determination, and to give our bird-watching one more chance, we placed another feeder on a tree branch outside the same living room window.

Imagine our surprise one evening at dusk when Mr. Bear was climbing the tree. My husband, instead of grabbing a camera, headed for the porch. As he stared at our guest, I heard him saying, "What do you think you're doing?" I don't know what kind of a response he was expecting, but I guess the bear was just as puzzled as I was when he made a hasty retreat ... to our neighbor's handy feeders once again.

**JUDY FREED** PUNXSUTAWNEY, PA

# Visitation by June and Family

WE LIVE IN THE EAGLES NEST LAKE area where the gentle bear June made periodic visits to our yard. Our bird feeder hung on a heavy cable between two cedar trees. June would climb one of the trees and beat on the cable to get the bird feeder swinging and bouncing. After the sunflower seeds flipped out of it, she would climb down and lie beneath the feeder and feast on them. One day her three cubs played all about her, climbing the trees and even trying to nurse while she ate. Later she walked down to the lake and while she was drinking, the cubs played in our yard. Cal and Bud were rolling about together looking like one big furball. All at once Lily spied them and ran across the yard. She jumped right on top of her brothers, and all three cubs rolled apart in three different directions. Indeed, it was a very funny sight. The only reason I knew that Lily was the cub that jumped on her brothers was because Sue Mansfield said, "That is what Lily would do." Bears have different personalities and Sue has certainly witnessed that.

On another day June put her cubs up a large red pine beside our driveway and then walked away. She was gone a long time and finally the cubs fell asleep with legs dangling down on either side of the limbs of the tree. They looked so cute up there but eventually we began to worry. What if they fell off the branch while sleeping? Why was June gone so long? Was she going to come back and get them? After about 45 minutes she appeared and in her bear way told them it was time to come down the tree. For some reason they refused to come down even with all her urgings. Finally, she started up the tree and I guess they got the message. They quickly descended and off they went together. We have enjoyed bears visiting our yard for years but now our barking yellow lab keeps them away. We miss seeing them up-close now.

**PAT JORDAN** ELY, MN

# Grizzles in the Yard, the Boat, the Camp

**WE HAVE HAD MANY GRIZZLIES** in our yard, so we are very careful with garbage and dog food and seeds. They love sunflower seeds and dry corn and anything that smells sweet. The last time we had a bear in our yard was last year. It had two cubs, and I think it is the same sow (and cubs) we have seen before. They come to a little spring that bubbles out of the hill in our backyard. Last summer a cub got in our big boat; it must have bumped the knob on the radio (it was on full volume. We had it on while we were running) and got scared. They sprinted away and were last seen at the Chatanika Lodge parking lot about four miles away.

We have learned that the bears are not afraid of fire. We had a bear drop into our camp (at Lake Mansfield near Tok, Alaska), walk into our tent and then go to the campfire and pick out the orange juice containers that were smoldering (I had just tossed them in the fire). The bear came by and we jumped into the boat. We saw 15 different bears in one day and night; they were cinnamon-colored black bears. We watched a mama with two babies eating duck eggs on the shore and her two-year-old cub sitting like a dog, watching. Mama seriously beat up a young male that ventured too close. That little male quickly ran up a 500-yard hill and sat behind a birch tree, thinking he was hiding. It was comical to watch. He would poke his head around the tree to see where the mama was. We dropped anchor and slept on the boat, not in the tent.

**LOIS SANNES** FAIRBANKS, AK

# Dinner at Five

**BEFORE WE MOVED TO THE NORTH** Georgia mountains, we had heard all the usual stories and warnings about black bears and felt cautious, but not really afraid. We knew we had to keep all food shut away and we couldn't have bird feeders hanging from poles in the yard the way we were accustomed to in Middle Georgia. So I had the builder put a "bird" deck on 20-foot steel poles where I could hang feeders. Since there were no steps up to the deck, we figured we didn't have to be concerned, since surely a bear couldn't climb up a tall, smooth pole like that.

We moved in during late spring, and one summer afternoon, we came upstairs to find one of the cats sitting in an open window staring intently at the bird deck. I thought, "How nice! She's enjoying watching the birds." Then I looked onto the deck where I saw a large black bear lying on the three-inch-wide deck railing, happily eating out of the bird feeder. I immediately ran to get my camera and took a few shots through the window and glass door leading out to the deck. My husband and our dog were also watching her, not two feet away, separated only by glass. I went down to the lower deck landing and began taking pictures. That's when I saw two small cubs wandering around at the base of the tall poles. But the mother bear didn't seem to be at all concerned that I was only about 15 feet from her and her cubs, snapping photos. Finally, she apparently decided she needed to supply her cubs with some food, so she took the feeder in her jaws and carried it down the pole, walking with the bottom of her back feet braced on the pole and her upper paws wrapped around it. She dropped the feeder on the ground, where the seed spilled, and she and her cubs ate the rest. I was too enchanted to be afraid at the time. Since then we have seen bears regularly and my experience taking a Black Bear Field Study Course at the Wildlife Research Institute in Ely convinced me I had nothing to fear from them. But we did extend our fence with the electric wire on top of it to keep the bears from hauling off all the feeders.

They've been very respectful of that barrier, and we very much enjoy having them around.

**JANICE EDENS** JASPER, GA

# What a Dump!

IT WAS THE SUMMER OF 1970. Like every summer, our family made its way up to the "North Shore" at least once. That year, we stayed near Grand Marais and we thought this would be a great time to take our children to see the bears at the Tofte dump. (My mother and father had taken me there years ago.)

As we drove slowly into the "dump" area, we started seeing bears. We felt the kids come from the back of the station wagon to the second seats. Soon we were surrounded by bears. It was wonderful. They were harmless, just looking for a good meal. A mama bear came with her three cubs. All at once she let out a loud call and all three cubs scurried up a nearby tree.

Then we saw the *big* Papa coming into the area. Soon our son leapt over the front seat and huddled under the dashboard. We assured him that as long as we stayed in the car, we would be fine. Now the "dump" is closed. I guess that is necessary, but our family enjoyed the bears of Tofte dump!

**SHARON HULTGREN** DASSEL, MN

# Bear in the Grapes

**I GREW UP IN A HUNTING FAMILY.** My brother and I had been in the woods with our dad from an early age. Eventually, we ended up with sons one year apart. Some of most fun I've had in my life has been bringing those boys up hunting and enjoying the outdoors. One year during a fall turkey hunt, both boys and I ended up at what we call "The Poplar," a yellow poplar tree approximately four feet in diameter that is about halfway up the mountain. It was a warm November day and none of us had heard anything so we sat there talking a while, then got out our turkey calls to see if we could stir something up. With a 14-year-old and 13-year-old, it wasn't long before they were just making a racket. All at once my son Stephen's eyes popped open and he said, "There's a bear." We looked up the hill but they were out of sight by then. He said it was a sow and cub and pointed to where they had been.

I told them to go up there and see if they could find a track. They started up the hill. They finally made it to where the bear had been, and I could see them checking the ground for sign. I heard something in the leaves to my left and looked in that direction to see a dark object moving through the woods. At first I thought it was a turkey, but it was a bear cub, probably seventy pounds and round as a tick. It moved toward me, then cut hard to the left. I thought it had seen me. The next thing I knew it was climbing a large oak tree twenty yards away. It went up about six feet, stopped and leaned back looking straight up the tree. It stayed there about four seconds, then came back down. Soon it was out of sight and I thought it was gone. The boys were in their own world by then and I couldn't get their attention. There was a shot around the mountain where my brother should have been so I yelled to the boys, "The bear is down here." Before the words had left my mouth, I heard limbs cracking and bark scraping and here comes the sow dropping out of a tree like a fireman on the brass pole. It hit the ground with a thud and was gone.

The boys came down and I told them my story. We looked at the claw marks and noticed that the tree had grapevines, still full of grapes. She had come around to feed on grapes and the cub had been checking the tree before it climbed up. We decided to head around the mountain to see if there were turkeys trying to get back together. Stephen had moved through the woods quietly and sat down for awhile. All at once he heard something. Here came another cub sliding down, not ten feet away. It had been up the tree eating grapes when Stephen sat down, then it decided enough was enough—it was time to go.

**DAVID JENKINS** ROANOKE, VA

# Bears in the Berries

IT WAS A SUNNY AFTERNOON in July 2009 in Wisconsin's north woods. I decided to pedal my bike some three miles to the nearby village, which held a Farmer's Market on Thursday afternoons. As I was meandering along the shoulder of Hwy 13, I noticed a black blur in the corner of my eye. "What was that?" I asked myself. "A critter, or just my imagination?" Hesitating, my pedaling slowed. Not sure, I decided to circle back and have a look. I crossed the highway and rode a little ways back. Just as I was about to stop the bike, there, in the middle of a lush raspberry patch only a few yards away, up popped a black bear! I stood still, watching Mr. Bear as Mr. Bear watched me. After a few seconds, the bear turned and trotted up out of the ditch and off to the thick woods. At the edge of the woods, he stopped and turned around, as if to look at me one more time. Instantly, up popped his friend (his sibling, perhaps?), from the same raspberry patch! Bear No. 2 looked at me, then turned and looked at Bear No. 1; he almost seemed to shrug as he plopped back down, landing on his behind, and resumed feasting on the bountiful berry buffet. I stood still, watching in amusement. Soon, Bear No. 1 seemed to get the reassurance he needed; he trotted back to the ditch, plopped himself down, and joined his pal in the berry patch. It was truly a delight to see these youngsters enjoying themselves! Cars continued to whiz by, wholly unaware, as I stood on the shoulder, gazing at this snippet of a day in the life of these dear north woods neighbors. Had I not been on my bike, traveling at 10 mph on the shoulder, I would have missed the whole show. There's something sweet about life in the slow lane.

ANN BODENSTEINER EDINA, MN

# Such a Gift

IT WAS ON A TRIP TO THE NORTH SHORE of Lake Superior, near Lake Nipigon, that we came upon a sow bear and three cubs in a mountain ash tree. We sat in the truck observing, enjoying, and snapping many pictures from only 30 feet away. Particularly fascinating was the way the mother would take a cluster of berries in her lips and carefully strip off only the ripest berries (much the same way I would pick blueberries!). She would break branches to make the berries more accessible to herself and the cubs. It was such a gift to watch them for perhaps a half hour before they melted into the woods again. Such a gift.

On the way home to the Upper Peninsula of Michigan we stopped in Ely on a rainy fall day. There we visited the North American Bear Center. After years of living in bear country, my view of bears was utterly transformed by that four-hour visit. I had always been taught to fear bears and rather dreaded meeting them when I was out on foot in the woods. But after that visit and after reading all the displays, fear just melted away. And later that winter, Hope was born ...

**ELIZABETH ROGERS TILLER, PHD** IRON RIVER, MI

# Smoky Bears

MY FAMILY HAS BEEN VISITING the Great Smoky Mountains National Park in Tennessee since the 1950s, and this area was my parents' favorite vacation spot. In my 40 years, I've been there close to 30 times. It was always the highlight of the trip if you were able to see a bear, and I've been lucky enough to see quite a few over the years, and in the 1980s, I even had a bologna sandwich stolen from my picnic table by a bear.

In 2005, my second husband went with me and my daughter on his first trip to the park. I was so hopeful that he would get to see a bear on his first trip, but there were plenty of trips where I didn't see any, so I didn't get my hopes up too much. We were driving through my favorite spot in the park, Cades Cove, and sure enough, I saw a bear walking towards the road in front of our car. I spotted it first and grabbed his arm—I was so excited for him and my daughter that I couldn't get the words out. They spotted it too and the bear walked between two cars in front of us and wandered away.

Last summer (August 2009), my husband, daughter and I made another trip to the area. We were driving the Cades Cove loop again, hopeful we would get to see another bear. Sure enough, a few miles into the loop, cars were pulling off the side of the road and people were getting out of their cars—a pretty good sign that a bear must be around. We parked the car and walked over to the trees where everyone else was and sure enough, a bear was up in the tree eating berries. There had to be at least 50 people standing there watching it and taking pictures, but this bear seemed oblivious to it all and moved from branch to branch as if no one was around. It was so wonderful to watch a wild bear doing what bears do. My daughter, who was ten years old at the time, asked me what we would do if he came out of the tree. Should we run? I told her that I've seen several bears over the years and not once did I feel threatened or scared. Now, I'm not one of the fools that I've seen who go right up to a bear and get close to take pictures, but I've never felt like I was in any danger. After twenty minutes or so, the bear was still up in the tree and we decided to move on, but that was not our last bear encounter! We also saw another mother bear and three cubs high in the trees as we drove through the loop. In fact, we were lucky enough to see a total of ten bears on that trip. It was awesome!

I feel like I've learned so much about bears in the last couple of months. I've never seen a bear while hiking through the Great Smoky Mountains, but last summer we did see signs posted on the trail to Grotto Falls that bears were active in the area. I wondered to myself what we would do if we encountered one, but I feel like I've learned enough through Lynn Rogers that a bear isn't going to come up behind us and attack us. I think I will be able to hike there in the future and not feel like I need to constantly be on the lookout for a bear. I'm sure that I would be nervous if we came upon one, but now I know that a bear won't be a threat.

**SUSAN DAVEY** LIBERTY TOWNSHIP, OH

# Extra Large Chipmunk

AT OUR SUMMER CABIN in Ontario, just north of Baudette, Minnesota, we see bears fairly often. Some years ago some friends brought over fruit. I tossed the nectarines out by the steps for the chipmunks. About an hour later there was a black bear lying on his belly, paws out, rolling and trying to munch a difficult nectarine. He reminded me of a dog with a yummy bone.

MARY ANN HENDON AKRON, OH

# Never too Young

MY VERY FIRST BEAR ENCOUNTER occurred when I was four years old, and from then on, I was hooked. My grandparents ran a YMCA family recreation camp called Deer Valley in Western Pennsylvania. We spent many days and nights in the woods of the Allegheny Mountains.

On a warm day in July of 1961, I was sitting on the front porch of our cabin and noticed some movement in the trees about 20 yards away. Out walked a large black bear from behind the trees. The bear was foraging. I was fascinated! I could not take my eyes off this beautiful creature. I called to my grandmother, who quietly joined me on the porch. We sat for about an hour, just watching and talking quietly. The bear would occasionally look up at us, then continue its mission of daintily eating various plants and grasses. It occurred to me that the bear did not care that we were there. It clearly knew we were there and that we meant no harm. My grandmother had spent so much time in the woods that to her, a bear was just part of the surroundings and nothing to be feared.

As we sat watching this beautiful big healthy black bear, she explained to me that the bears were here first. Grandma Gladys told me that we needed to respect their home in the woods. Perhaps because my grandmother did not fear the bear that day, I learned not to fear them, but to respect them, and revere their existence and presence. Both my grandparents were way ahead of their time in their views about nature, conservation and bears. I truly thank them both for this. Thanks to them, I have never felt afraid in the woods or feared bears, and I have been fortunate to see a few more bears during my camping days. I treasure each encounter for the true gift it is. Never has a bear given me cause for fear or mistrust. I keep my distance, I respect the bear's space and let the bear go about its day. I thank my grandmother and that beautiful black bear in 1961 that gave me the privilege of watching him.

**CYNTHIA WULKAN-FONTANE** PUTNAM VALLEY, NY

# Bird Feeder Dining

MY SON, WHO LIVES 80 miles north of the Twin Cities, always puts out feeders for the birds. On one afternoon last winter (2009), they looked out their sliding doors to see a black bear at the feeding station a short distance from the door. I viewed the video they took and it was amazing. The black bear appeared to be a young bear, and he/she was alone at this time. My son's wife and daughter walked out to see the bear. They approached very slowly and were able to get within 50 feet of this young bear. The young bear didn't seem to mind being admired. I explained some of the bear behavior I have learned from the wonderful people at the North American Bear Center. I wish everyone could understand bears and live with them in harmony. This bear just wanted to eat and didn't feel threatened.

**DIANE L. JOHNSON** WOODBURY, MN

# A Vanquished Fear

**WE LIVE IN THE MOUNTAINS** in Virginia so bear encounters are frequent at times. My first encounter after moving here occurred when I was on the four-wheeler going along a creek to feed the horses. There was a mountain and creek on my left side and a mountain on my right side. My husband was riding with me and he yelled in my ear, "BEAR!" He wasn't concerned; he just wanted me to see it. I, on the other hand, was terrified. (I was raised in grizzly country and when someone yelled, "Bear," you didn't stop to look at it. Good thing those type of bears were always in the distance so we had time to get away). Anyway, back to the story in Virginia. I screamed so loud the bear looked to his left (the echo had startled him), and he turned and ran straight for us. I froze and couldn't move and he went by me so fast the four-wheeler just shook (my husband says it was me shaking). The poor thing is probably in another county by now and will probably never come near humans again.

Along this same road my husband came across a cub not more than 15-20 pounds. It was sitting in a blackberry bush raking the berries with both paws. Jim was on a tractor, so he didn't have his camera with him. He came up to the house and we went back down on the four-wheeler to get a picture and the mama bear had taken her cub up the mountain behind our house. The creek is where they go to get water and then they head back up the mountain. They tend to live behind us instead of on the other side of the mountain because of the bear hunters that hunt with dogs. We don't allow hunting on our property, so I think that is the reason the bears feel safer on this side.

This year (2009) we planted a cornfield below our house (it was usually alfalfa hay). When we were ready to harvest, the very center of this cornfield was the new living area for the bears. The mama bear demolished the entire center of the cornfield and let me tell you, she waddled into hibernation this year. She had to walk right by our house to get to the creek. Never once did we see her or hear her. It was a scary feeling knowing she was there every day camping 100 feet from us. Late in October Jim stood below a tree and heard something above his head and there was a cub eating wild grapes while sitting on a tree branch. He took some pictures with his cell phone and the cub continued to eat with no concern whatsoever. Jim talked to him as he was taking pictures and was totally ignored the entire time. We never did see his mama.

The folks at the North American Bear Center have helped me overcome my fear of the bears. I am not saying I will run up to one and try to pet it, but I will not scream and scare it to death either. They can continue to live very peacefully behind our house.

**GRACIA LAM** TOUCHOWEST FARM, MOUNT SOLON, VA

# Not a Lab

IN 1994, I MOVED to Snoqualmie, Washington. My lot borders many acres of undeveloped land. During the first summer, I looked out my window and saw what I thought was a black lab at the back of my lot. I went out to say hello, but was surprised to find that it was black bear eating the blackberries. The bear turned and saw me. We both ran, the bear ran into the woods, and I ran into the house. I was so excited that I lived in a place where I could see a bear in my yard.

Last summer, I found my neighbor's trash bag shredded in the same place I had seen the bear years before. After seeing the scat, I was sure it was a bear. I was hopeful that I could spot it again. Several weeks later, around four in the morning, I heard my recycling bin fall over. I got up to look and saw a very large black bear walk right by my front door. I was so happy to see it. I had picked up trash on the road near my house and had forgotten that it was in the trunk of my car. Some of the trash included food waste from restaurants. When I got up in the morning, instead of little cat feet on my car, I had big bear prints everywhere. There were even nail marks on my bumper. Even so, I was happy to see the bear and even happier that my trunk was not ripped open.

**CHRISTINA SORENSEN** SNOQUALMIE, WA

# Bear
# Behavior

# FICTION:

Bears are totally unpredictable.

# FACT:

With study, bear behavior can be predicted.

Black bear behavior varies because bears are intelligent animals with individual personalities. If people are unfamiliar with black bears, it can make them seem unpredictable. But the researchers at the North American Bear Center have been walking with wild black bears for the last quarter century, and they have found black bear behavior to be highly predictable. Each bear has its own personality, but no bear attacked any of the researchers or hurt them. On the contrary, the bears consistently avoided conflict. By learning the truth about black bears, people can view black bears for what they are and better enjoy hiking and living in bear country.

# The Nonchalance of Bears

ON OUR TRIP to the Great Smoky Mountains in 2009, we went to Cades Cove and saw black bears. We stood under an oak tree and watched a mother bear and her four cubs eat acorns up in the tree. There were probably a hundred people watching this awesome sight. It was phenomenal. On another visit in 2010 we were hiking and saw a lone male yearling walking past us; we stopped to watch him, he looked at us and sniffed the air and kept on walking. We were not scared thanks to the education that Dr. Rogers provided. We respected them and they ignored us.

TOM AND JEAN BUSHNELL WAPAKONETA, OHIO

# My First Bear Encounter

I MET MY FIRST BEAR in the middle of the night. It stood over me so closely I could have touched it, but I couldn't see it.

Three of us were camped beside the Little Two-hearted River in Michigan's Upper Peninsula. We had pitched a tent where a high trestle bridge crossed the river. The tent seemed small, so I put my air mattress out under the stars and crawled under a blanket. Mosquitoes and no-see-ums were keeping me awake, so I pulled the blanket up over my face. About midnight, I went on alert under the blanket as footsteps approached from the woods. That's when I realized I was in bear country. I didn't know what to do. I didn't dare move as it sniffed my feet, worked its way up to my face, and intently sniffed the blanket over my face. It then stepped around my head, walked a few steps, and tipped over a garbage can. I'd always heard that bears were dangerous, but nothing about the gentle sniffing felt that way.

The next evening, the bear was back. I don't know why I reacted like I did, but as we drove in and saw the bear near our tent, I threw open the door and ran after it. I chased it as long as I could hear it crashing away in the woods, but when the woods went quiet, I looked into the darkening shadows and turned back.

The next morning, I was fishing waist deep in the river when something caught my eye swimming toward me. It was near the bank, big and partially obscured by protruding alder branches. It kept coming. I was sorry I'd chased the bear. I hoped it wasn't mad. Twenty feet away, it climbed the bank—a beaver.

Fifty-five years later, I still remember how fear affected my thoughts about bears on that trip. Knowing that about myself has helped me interpret the behaviors of the bears I've studied these past 44 years. It helped me to interpret their behavior in terms of their fear, rather than my fear, and learn more about what drives them than otherwise would have been possible.

**LYNN ROGERS** ELY, MN

# A Little Snack

IT WAS MEMORIAL DAY WEEKEND of 2008 and we were sitting out around the campfire when about 30 yards behind us we heard some snorts and huffing sounds. There was no exchange of looks; everyone just jumped up and ran FAST! Of course, having cabins up north (Webster,

WI), we know we live among the animals. Anyway, once inside I realized I still had my glass of wine, untipped! And then we saw the bear. She had two small cubs with her, which she sent up a tree. She proceeded to pull down the bird feeder, and its glass ball landed on her head. When that happened, she scrambled up the tree. Once she realized there was no danger, she came back down and ate all the seed. Then she walked down to the lake and finally came back up and left with her babies. We took screens out of the windows and snapped a bunch of pictures, and she was unfazed by it all. She was a beautiful bear with that very distinct "V" on her chest. We have seen plenty of bears since then.

**ANDREA LARSON** ST. PAUL, MN

# Something Fishy Is Going On!

**MY FIRST CAMPING TRIP** was in the Adirondack Mountains in New York. I was with my husband, another couple and their infant daughter. Our friends were experienced hikers and campers. We chose an isolated campsite along a beautiful lake. There was a narrow, wooden footbridge over a small creek that led to our car. While we were setting up our tents, we saw a group of children walking down the road clapping sticks together. I assumed they were playing, but later found out that they were trying to keep bears away! After our tents were up, we noticed a black bear a few feet away at the edge of the woods. He was standing there watching us! He watched for a while and then left. As a city girl, I was very concerned about that bear. No one mentioned bears would be joining us on this camping trip. We reported our bear sighting to the park ranger who assured us that we had nothing to worry about. He said that a black bear would not harm us.

The following day the guys went fishing and the ladies enjoyed each other's company, took in the sun and enjoyed the beautiful scenery. After a delicious fish dinner, we took a short ride to the garbage dump where we watched black bears eating and sometimes competing for food. One very large bear came out of the woods from behind us and walked across the parking lot to the dump. At the sight of this bear, many of us ran into cars … the closest car to where we were standing. The bear paid no attention to us and just walked past the cars and people. I continued to watch this bear from inside someone else's car until the bear went down the hill to the dump. I was amazed that he and the other bears paid no attention to us.

Later, we returned to the campground, which did not have electricity. After our long day we settled into our sleeping bags, in our little two-man tents, with our flashlights in hand. Sometime during the night I was awakened by a noise outside our tent. It sounded very close. I also heard the loud voices of our friends. I struggled to get out of my sleeping bag and to unzip the tent. As I exited the tent, I could see nothing but total darkness. The noise I was hearing was the tumbling of our cooler that had the fish the guys had caught earlier in the day. This bear had come for a midnight snack! I tried to make my way to my car, but in the darkness I could not see the little bridge that led the way. By the time I got into my car, the bear and fish were gone. Not knowing much about bears and being really scared by this too-close encounter, I spent the rest of my nights sleeping in my car.

I have learned so much from watching and reading about Lily, Hope and the other research bears. I now have a better understanding of their behavior and no longer believe that black bears are the vicious animals I once thought they were. Many thanks to Dr. Rogers for sharing his research and teaching me the truth about black bears.

**MARY O'BRIEN** NEW CITY, NY

# Camping with Bears

**SEVERAL YEARS AGO** in early June we arrived at our annual fishing camp destination near Ignace, Ontario, and were met with the news that bears were in camp. The new owner of the camp was trying desperately to get a mother bear and two small cubs removed because they were becoming a nuisance. Daily calls to the Ministry failed to produce any results. In an attempt to scare them off, the owner set off so many firecrackers it sounded like we were in a war zone. The last straw came when the guests in one of the cabins left their fish-fry leftovers from the night before, including the fish-frying grease, in the kitchen sink. Mama bear and both cubs were seen breaking and entering through a window that had been left open and that looked far too small to allow their entry. Now guests were scared. The owner put in another call to the Ministry and told them that if they didn't get the bears out of camp, he would have to shoot them, and he did not want to do that. Finally, a female official arrived with a large trap that she baited with food. Mama bear was the first to be trapped, then one cub. But catching the second cub proved to be more difficult. It would climb on top, go around and around the trap trying to get to its mother, but it took the entire day to finally trap it. We were told by the official that if the second cub was not captured, she would have to release Mama bear and the one cub because they could not break up the family. I was getting very concerned because Mama bear was frantic and we all felt so sorry for her. She calmed down when she was finally reunited with both cubs. The officer told us that she was relocating the family to an area approximately 60 miles away where there was an ideal spot for them with a stream running through it. Everyone in the camp was relieved that the bears were safely and humanely removed. Of course, I knew nothing about black bears back then. But I do know that many in the camp were concerned for them, including the owner, and we were all very pleased with the resolution.

**DONNA HOUSE** TOWNSEND, WI

# Camp Richardson Campground

SEVERAL YEARS AGO a friend and I decided to spend a summer night camping at Camp Richardson in South Lake Tahoe, California. It was a last-minute decision so we went with little more than a tent, bedding, an ice chest, and mostly for the ambience, an old metal cowboy coffee pot. We had no means of cooking, so the evening meal consisted of a trip to the market and a smorgasbord of snacks ranging from jars of oysters to packages of Twinkies. Oh, and Rolaids too!

There were signs posted at the campground advising that black bears and raccoons frequented the area so food should be stored away securely. We put the remnants of our feast in the trunk of the car. As we crawled in the tent, I brought the old metal coffee pot and a stick with me, and I jokingly said it was going to be my "bear alarm."

Late in the night we had a visitor! I woke up to the sound of something big close to the tent on the side I was sleeping. It was close enough that I could hear husky breathing and sniffing, and I could detect its movement along the tent's edge. Bear! I immediately woke my tentmate. I was fearful. Even though we had no food in the tent, I was afraid the bear might tear its way in and attack us. We could hear the bear makes its way toward the picnic table, but then it came back and again directed its attention to the tent. My fear was growing. I remembered the coffee pot and started banging on it with the stick and saying, "Go away bear, go away!"

All my noisemaking didn't seem to be much of a deterrent. We were trying to decide if we should stay in the tent, try to get out, or wait and see if the cell phone had reception to call for help. My heart was racing, and although I have always "loved" bears, I was truly terrified. Just when I thought my heart was going to beat out of my chest, I heard distant voices and the bark of a large dog. There was sudden activity. One side of the tent temporarily crushed in; there was a flurry of what sounded like pine needles and paws, and then quiet. The bear had left and did not return; it took quite some time for us to return to sleep after this encounter.

In the morning we found very clear paw prints in the camp dirt and on the back end of the car, where the bear had apparently smelled the snacks in the trunk. In reality, if the bear had wanted to get us, it could have easily come through the flimsy tent. The sight or sound of the other campers and the dog was enough to scare off the bear.

I have since learned more appropriate means of food storage when camping. Also, through the North American Bear Center, I have learned about black bear behavior and how they are mostly timid creatures. My love of bears is strong and my fear of them is now being replaced with understanding.

ALOHA MONTGOMERY PLACERVILLE, CA

# Barnaby Makes a Visit (or two)

WE WERE CAMPING near the Devils Cascade in the Boundary Waters Canoe Area. I crawled out of our tent, stood up, stretched, and looked around at the beautiful creation before me. There, just a few feet behind our tent sat a bear. He was sitting on his haunches, like a dog, just looking at me. My first impulse was to scream "BEAR!"; my second impulse was to dive back into the tent to get my camera. We all came scrambling back out of the tent making as much noise as we could . . . the bear was disappearing into the trees.

That night, we moved on to another campsite further down the trail. We had made our supper and had an unfortunate accident in that our pot full of supper had tipped over; much of it fell into the cooking fire. We made do with crackers and peanut butter that night, strung our food pack up between two trees and went to bed. We heard some noise in the middle of the night, a scraping and almost a sneezing sound. We dug around for our flashlight and saw "our" bear digging in the fire pit area, likely enjoying the burnt remains of our supper. I knew it was "our" bear because his nose was almost exactly half brown and half black. We banged some pots and pans and he decided that our "burnt offerings" were not worth the pain in his ears. We continued on to different sites for the next few days but came back and camped at Devils Cascade for our last night in the BWCA. "Our" bear came around again; he did not come very close, but we would see him in different spots near our campsite throughout the day. He was a perfect gentleman even though we did not have any "burnt offerings" for him. We named him Barnaby Bear and he is what we remember most about that trip to the BWCA.

**SANDY SWANSON** COON RAPIDS, MN

# Fishing with Bears

FISHING WAS SLOW AT SNAKE LAKE. But since this was our favorite spot to catch trout, we stayed a little longer than we should have. Dusk was approaching. I was fishing at the clearing. The car was nearby. As usual, my sister, Ursula, wandered off to find her own spot. She started fishing between the tall shrubs, about sixty feet to the left of me. We were the only two at the lake. Until I heard the splashing. I couldn't see anything, but just heard a lot of loud splashing near Ursula. I yelled to her several times, "I hear loud splashing." She answered, "It must be a dog." I looked around, but didn't see anything. It didn't sound like a dog in the water. The loud splat-splat-splat continued. Again, I shouted to her about the unusual loud splashing. A few minutes later, she finally came back to fish by me. As we were reeling in our fishing lines, getting ready to leave, I glanced to my left and got the surprise of my life. A black female bear came out of the exact spot where Ursula had been fishing just five minutes earlier. "Bear, Bear," I shouted! We dropped our fishing poles and jumped into the car. As we watched the big bear, along came her three little cubs. They headed for the dirt road, above the lake. The bears scampered off into the woods. We sat in the car, stunned and surprised. We were fishing with the bears and we didn't even know it. We don't know what the bears were doing. Maybe the mama bear was fishing, too. Or, maybe she was just taking her cubs to the lake for a drink and a dip.

It's been said that a bear can smell a human a mile away, and that a bear will either run and hide or tree her cubs if she senses the presence of people. I don't know why the bears stayed. I don't know why the bears decided to fish with us. All I know is that we were lucky, with our close encounter of the bear kind.

As I tell my young grandchildren the story of grandma fishing with the bears, I smile as they listen in awe.

**ROSEMARY TURNER** LAKEWOOD, CO

# The New Bear in Town

**IT WAS 3:00 A.M. ON A JULY MORNING** in 2004, and on Washington Avenue in Stevens Point, Wisconsin, residents were turning on porch lights. Neighbors were phoning other neighbors with surprising news: A black bear was balanced about 12 feet up in a magnificent old elm.

Located in the front yard of a city home, the elm had provided a firm seat to a frightened young bear. He had probably been pushed out of his mother's territory to find his own range. In all likelihood, the odors of the remnants of Friday night's fish fry emanating from a dumpster across the street caused him to wander into the urban area from the woods about one mile north. The inexperienced youngster had perhaps become confused and alarmed. And what do bears do when they are uneasy? Climb a tree! As residents arose that Saturday morning, word spread, bringing a crowd that grew with daylight. This almost certainly caused the bear, a small 140-pound, two-year-old male, to become even more terrified; he looked down over the crowd and seemed to shiver.

The longer he stayed in the elm, the more residents began to worry about him. This Saturday in July was hot and sunny, and his black, heavy fur had to be causing him to overheat. One neighbor stretched caution tape to keep gawkers at a distance, and eventually the police barricaded the road, with hopes that the bear would climb out of the tree and run away on his own. But the bear would not leave his perch.

Officials from the Wisconsin Department of Natural Resources had to use tranquilizer darts to sedate the adolescent, and then they removed him from the tree with a forklift. Once in a cage, he was transported to a secure location. Before being released in his new home, the youngster became alert, huffing and puffing, sounding like a fearsome creature; but in reality the sounds reflected his nervousness. Once out of the cage, he ran into the woods where hopefully he has made a safer life for himself, remaining wild and free.

**JAN AND KATHY HERMANN** STEVENS POINT, WI

# Bear Encounter

**WE HAVE A CABIN** in Presque Isle, Wisconsin. Every summer we take a two week vacation, and it never fails—for the last 10 years we've always seen the same black bear that comes to our deer feeder and bird feeders. The way we can tell it is the same bear is that she has a stiff back leg. We can't tell if it is broken or not but she can't bend it at all. She walks fine but you can definitely tell it's her. We have named her "Gimpy." Six years ago she came around with two cubs. They were born that year. It was so interesting to watch them. They played like little children. One day I went into the garage to get a good picture and when the camera flashed, she ran to the edge of the trees, stood on her back legs and grunted. The two cubs ran up the trees like lightning. I was sure scared and ran inside. We watched for a while as mom left and the cubs stayed in the trees. They eventually came down. We continue to see this same bear every year, and we look forward to seeing if she will come each year.

Three years later a bear came to our feeders with three cubs! We think the mother was one of Gimpy's offspring. It was so comical to see three cubs running around and playing. They came several nights in a row. I am always in awe when I see these beautiful black bears.

**FAITH BARAN** CARPENTERSVILLE, IL

# Waiting for Bear

**I LIVE ON THE COAST OF MAINE** in the woods on the side of a very small mountain called Ducktrap. This mountain and my land go down to a river called the Ducktrap River because long ago the Indians used to trap ducks there. This is a special river because it is one of only six that has a genetically pure strain of wild Atlantic salmon breeding in it. I spend a lot of time exploring both the river and the mountain. I track animals in the summer and winter to learn where they go and what they do. I also look for scat (animal poop) to see who has been walking in the woods, follow trails made by the deer and other animals (there are no human trails), and look for signs, like maple trees debarked by moose and deer and pine trees gnawed by porcupines. In the fall and winter I search for dropped antlers (sheds, as they are called).

I take a lot of pictures with motion-sensor cameras and I have a homemade, live-streaming camera with infrared light for night and day viewing so I can see what is happening at a feeding station up in the woods from my house. When I wake up in the middle of the night, I can check out what the animals are doing. I have even seen an owl swoop down to grab a little mouse quietly eating cracked corn.

I have several feeding stations in the woods. My house is in a deer yard, an area where deer congregate in winter to make a set of trails to follow to get to food through the deep snow. Sometimes I have up to forty deer around my house. I have moose, coyotes, bobcats, fisher, raccoons, weasels and even a bear.

It is this bear that I want to talk about. When I moved here, I really wanted to have a bear come to my house, but no one had seen a bear on this mountain for many years, not since the last big one was shot by a hunter. I had seen a bear twice along a town road. Both times the person I was with and I looked at each other and said, "That was a bear," followed by, "No, it couldn't have been." Both times I stopped the car and we peered into the woods but could see nothing. Back home, I looked and looked for tracks or scat in my woods with no luck. Everyone knew that I was hoping for a bear to come. "Have you seen your bear yet?" they asked (yet being the operant word).

Then, on the morning of June 13, I went up to check my digital camera at the feeding station where I had been watching raccoons on the live-feed camera all night. Looking in the little camera window, I saw a close-up of a very big coon. I brought the card from the camera down to my computer and checked it out. Wow, it wasn't a coon at all but a black bear that had arrived at 1:30 in the morning. The picture showed his eyes glowing in the light from the flash, and I guess he didn't like that much because he seems to have left without eating. I was sorry about that and put out all sorts of enticing food to encourage him to come back but, disappointingly, he never did.

I looked for that bear all summer until it was time for hibernation, and I started again in the spring. And then, on June 11, I looked out my window and there was the bear, this time right beside my house. I must have been on his June social calendar. He was standing there, swallowing the last of the suet from the suet feeder and beginning to eye a sunflower seed feeder that I had worked very hard to hang up. The window where I was standing was open and I said very softly, "Oh, please don't do that," as he reached for the seed. The bear stopped, looked up at me, looked at the feeder and then slowly and gently lowered his paw and walked off. I said a quiet "Thank you." I felt relieved that my feeder was safe but disappointed that the bear felt he had to leave. So, after a little while I went out and put a pile of sunflower seed on the ground for him, but he never returned and I never found a sign of him in the woods.

So, the next year I was looking forward to June, but on the morning of April 6, I checked a camera in my backyard and what did I find but a close-up picture of a bear rump! In looking around further, I could see that the bear had enjoyed birdseed, suet, deer feed and corn and apparently was quite happy because he was around again that night. I was so excited. I put out more good food as well as anise and molasses and the bear seemed impressed. He arrived at 8:00 p.m. and was still eating at midnight. I watched him for hours and had quite a one-way conversation with him. He seemed okay with this. The amazing thing was that there were a lot of dry leaves on the ground, and he was pretty big (some people suggested about 300–350 pounds), but when he walked and even ran I could not hear a sound. At one point I was so tired I asked if he would leave so that I could get some sleep since I could not tear myself away while he was visiting. He retreated for a few minutes but then was back. I went to bed anyway. I fell asleep for a little while and then woke up and when I opened my eyes and looked at the TV screen from the live-feed camera, there he was, enjoying snacks up there. He lay down for a while and napped and then sat up in the Buddha position and seemed quite content. He stayed around for two days and then was gone. I was disappointed but very excited when he returned in two weeks. He stayed another two days and then was gone, making that his final appearance despite all the home cooking I did to encourage his return.

Last year he did not come at all and I spent months watching and waiting, right up until the snow began. Now we are beginning another spring and I am again watching and waiting and hoping; I have some good snacks all ready for any bear that chooses to visit.

**CORELYN SENN** LINCOLNVILLE, ME

# The Fourth of July Bear

IT WAS EARLY MORNING on July 2, and I was preparing to make potato salad for our daughter's family who were to arrive that evening. It was tradition that they visited us at the lake every year for the Fourth of July celebrations. The morning was cool, with a nice breeze off the water, so I had opened the kitchen window and sliding patio door to allow the stuffy air out of the cabin. I was home alone. My husband and son are early golfers and had headed out to the course. Bacon was sizzling in the pan on the stove, and I would periodically step out on the deck to refill the small bird feeder. This feeder was posted into the ground and stood directly off the deck, only 3½ feet off the ground. Busy chipmunks kept jumping into the feeder, stuffing their cheeks and making off with the goods. They were certainly getting more seeds than the birds were.

I was on the fourth trip out to replenish the seed, when I heard a very distinct roar coming from the edge of the woods. My head snapped up, but

I could see no movement, and I could not hear any foliage rustling. Yet the roar had been close, perhaps 200 feet away. Odd, I thought, as I swiftly darted inside. I had never heard a bear vocalize, but was pretty certain that's what it was. Except for the breeze and the birds, all was quiet. I could hear a motor out on the water, but it was on the other side of the lake. I closed the door in an attempt to save my life.

We knew there were bears in these north woods of Minnesota, but people rarely saw them. I had seen only one bear, perhaps five years prior, and he was crossing the road a quarter-mile from my house. My in-laws had seen a bear in our yard late one night in the fall. I continued cooking, occasionally looking out the window. Nothing. No movement, no sound. Half an hour later the chipmunks were beginning to crawl up my screens, trying to get my attention, begging for food. "Well," I told myself, "whatever it was is gone. Unless it's circling around the house to ambush me as soon as I step out."

Cautiously I slid the door open and looked both ways before proceeding with the cup of seed six feet to the feeder. Sure enough, while pouring the seed in, I heard it again. Not a long roar, but a vocal roar. It came from the same area, just inside the edge of the woods. I slowly slid into the house and closed and locked the patio door. Shortly after, my husband and son arrived home from golf. The sound of the garage door going up was welcome music. I had decided not to say anything about the roar I had heard. The guys would make fun of me. I knew I'd never hear the end of it, and I'd be the butt of every joke all week. There is no way I'd mention the roar. Besides, whatever it was would be gone after hearing the car and the noisy garage door. I unlocked the door to let the guys in. "Why don't you have the door open, get some air in here?" My husband wanted to know. "It's beautiful out there!" So he left the door open. "What can I do to help?" he wanted to know.

"Well, I'd like to take a shower," I said as I put the potato salad in the fridge. "Would you dust the dining room chairs off?" After all, the family was arriving in only a few hours.

"Sure," he said.

The dining room is right off the kitchen, and the table and chairs are in front of a second patio door, leading to the same deck. It has a perfect view of the bird feeder. Shortly after my husband grabbed the furniture polish, I went to take my shower. No sooner had I gotten my hair wet when my son Justin was knocking on the bathroom door. "Mom! Mom, it's a bear! There's a bear in the yard! Hurry! Water off, throw on robe, grab a towel." I ran into the main room.

My husband said, "You missed him."

Here's what happened: While my husband was dusting the chairs, something outside caught his eye. Before he turned his head, he thought it was a large dog. But once he looked, he saw it was a bear, and it was only about 12 feet away! The bear, George estimates, weighed roughly 200 pounds, and had walked directly up to the little bird feeder I had been putting seed in. The bear looked in it, pushed it around with his snout, saw it was empty and gave it up. He looked around the rest of the yard. The bear may have seen George's movement through the window, because he suddenly ran like a bullet through the yard to the opposite side of the cabin. I didn't see a thing! But I was able to tell my husband and son, "I heard him! When you were gone I heard him roar!"

They both looked at me. "Sure you did."

Had the bear been attracted by the smell of bacon through my window? Had he seen me put something in the feeder and watched the birds and chipmunks come to eat? Why did he twice make vocal sounds? Had someone else been feeding him, and he knew this behavior but was leery of me?

As far as we know, this little bear never returned. Through the years we have occasionally seen bears in the yard. One night a large female with a yearling and a small cub inspected our styrofoam minnow bucket. Another night, a large female walked through, followed by three cubs. But we go years between bear sightings. I've always been afraid of meeting a bear while I was outside. But since I've discovered Lynn and the North American Bear Center, and his research findings, I feel so much more comfortable. The thought of meeting a bear no longer scares me.

**PAULA ANN BARDAHL** BATAVIA, IL

# Bears Just Want to Have Fun

**THIS HAPPENED SEVERAL YEARS AGO**, but it will forever be a cherished memory.

We had set up a tetherball pole for our kids; it was embedded in concrete. One afternoon our two dogs, who were in the house, started barking. Upon inspection from our window, we observed five black bears: a mother and four cubs—two cubs and two yearlings. The mother definitely gave the cubs a message to go up a nearby tree. The two smaller ones did as she requested, but the other two were determined to play tetherball. They actually stood up and hit the tetherball back and forth to each other. Mom was not pleased that they didn't pay attention to her, so she walked over to the tetherball and knocked the whole thing out of the ground (cement and all). Needless to say, the youngsters decided mom was serious and made tracks for the tree. She made another sound and they all climbed down the tree. We watched as they all walked back into the woods behind our house. I so wish we had pictures. We were all so engrossed with this fabulous wildlife experience, we didn't even think of a camera until after the fact.

**MARY JANE KUHLMEY** DULUTH, MN

# No, Sarge, No

I **LIVE IN A VERY RURAL COUNTY** where black bear sightings were typical and we've seen many around the house we have built. So, I've watched them for a long time. My current dog, Sarge, is a chaser. I hate that, but he's a chaser when it comes to bear. My husband was 500 yards down the drive tending the garden, and I was up near the house tending my flower gardens just at the woods' edge. Sarge had been with my husband in the garden looking for mice. While I was tending my flowers, I heard a stick crack in the woods. I knew it was a bear but by this time, I was more comfortable with them to know that it would not just come out of the woods and attack me so I continued weeding the beds. In no time, my dog was in the woods barking a "bear bark." I knew the bark and knew what the story was. So I grabbed whatever I had (in this case it was a shovel) and followed his barks. I was more concerned for the dog and put *all* fear that I may have had of bears aside, and in the woods I went calling for Sarge with shovel in hand. I was so concerned that the bear would swat at him. He's been a very lucky dog when it comes to bears. I came out of the deeper woods onto our trail to see the bear cross the trail with Sarge chasing a little way behind it. My husband, hearing the bear bark, came up and called for him. The bear made it to the high field grass and stood up looking for Sarge. We finally managed to have Sarge come to us and the bear meandered away. We scolded Sarge, as a bear is the last thing we want him to chase.

Just this past summer, we've had one bear in particular visit us; he was scoping out the sunflower seeds in a trash can on the porch. This was dumb on our part so we moved the can to our laundry room inside. The bear was a frequent visitor. My sister came up for a five-day visit. She has not been

**74**

up for many years and was an early riser. One morning when it was barely light, I heard the bear at the bird feeder as Sarge ran down the stairs. So, of course, I got up and realized that the back door had slammed shut! My sister let Sarge out of the house! I ran down the stairs, and couldn't believe she had let him out. She is not as country smart as I thought. I ran out to my car for my .38 Special. I knew the sound of gunshot would bring Sarge off the bear. It worked, but not before all our hearts were pounding. I didn't want to scare away the bear nor did I want Sarge to get swatted. I certainly let my sister know that in this neck of the woods, one does not let a dog out of the house without looking around first. She learned her lesson.

I truly look forward to running into a bear or two, especially now after being a daily visitor and a den cam observer the past year. That's not to say that my heart does not still pound when I encounter one, but when I see them, it's with great admiration and respect. From a distance, I truly love these creatures. I have many pictures taken in a hurry . . . as you may have guessed.

SUZI OWENS TIOGA, PA

# A Close Encounter on Lake Vermilion

SOME YEARS AGO, my wife and I were vacationing with my sister and her family at a resort on Minnesota's Lake Vermilion. My brother-in-law and I had been out fishing until after dark one evening, and when we returned to our cabin, we discovered that the girls and the children were not there. Assuming they were taking a sauna, we walked quietly down a wooded path in the moonlight to find them. Since our eyes were adjusted to the darkness and we knew the way, we hadn't turned on our flashlights. As we came around the back of a service truck parked near some outbuildings, however, we failed to discern the black silhouettes of a large sow with no less than four cubs standing directly in our path. By the time we sensed they were there, we had nearly stumbled over the sow. I had never been so close to a bear in my life, and I feared that by startling her and the cubs, we could be in real danger.

The scene abruptly came to a screeching halt as we stopped in our tracks and the cubs treed, screaming in fear. We quickly switched on our flashlights and shone them on the sow, who blinked in the glare and began to turn away, looking for an escape route. At the same time, the cubs' bawling had alerted the people in the cabin directly behind her, and suddenly a porch light came on and a man emerged, shouting for his family to come see the bears.

I will never forget that moment as long as I live. Everything seemed to shift into slow motion and I swore I could read the thoughts of the sow. She assessed the yelling man who blocked her escape and then, lowering her head ominously, turned back to glare at us, as if to say, "It looks like the only way out is through you." My heart leapt into my throat and I froze, trying to think of what we should do. My brother-in-law whispered that we should run for the flatbed truck behind us, but I was sure that would provoke a predatory response, like running from a threatening dog. In the grip of terror, I instinctively began speaking to the bear in a calm, soothing tone. "That's a good bear," I cooed. "We're not going to hurt you." Her response was less than encouraging: She raised her hackles and chuffed loudly, expelling air from her nose and mouth. The cubs' screams from above sounded to me like an admonition—"Kill them quickly, Mommy,

**76**

and let's get out of here!" We started to slowly back away from the animal, keeping our lights trained on her eyes so she couldn't get a bead on us. The bear clacked her jaws and stiffened, slapping the ground. I was now certain that we would be attacked at any second.

When we had put several feet of space between ourselves and the bear, we lowered our lights to allow her to see that there was, in fact, another way out, off to her side. She looked up to the trees where the cubs were clinging and gave some unheard signal, prompting them to shinny down in an instant. Then, they bounded off into the shadows, leaving us standing there with our hearts pounding in the cool night air.

For years, I relished telling the harrowing tale of the time we were nearly eaten by a menacing black bear in the north woods. I never stopped to think that I was actually projecting my fears onto her. After visiting the North American Bear Center and learning more about bear behavior, I've come to see the encounter through the sow's eyes and now realize that she was probably far more frightened than we were that night. Surprised and cornered as she was, she actually showed amazing restraint, despite her size and power. She was simply doing what any protective mother would do when confronted with a threat: looking for the quickest way out of the situation and trying to keep her family safe. While it doesn't sound quite as impressive to tell people about the time I scared a poor mother bear and her four cubs out of their wits, I take satisfaction in finally knowing the truth about bears and the ways that they relate to humans.

**TOM JANEWAY** GURNEE, IL

# A Special Encounter

IN THE SUMMER OF 2009, my husband and I were blessed to be a part of the healing process for a very special two-year-old bear whom we named Benson. As we had known Benson's mother, Clara, for several years, she had become comfortable around us and brought her cubs for frequent visits.

We got to watch Benson (who was born in January 2007) grow up. Clara gave him "the boot" in the summer of 2008 when she was ready to mate again. With his new independence, Benson expanded his territory, and we saw him less and less ... until July of 2009 when he showed up at our home in the north woods hobbling on three legs. It was obvious that his front paw had been caught in a snare. He was able to pull it off, but it left his paw mangled and infected.

On the advice of a wildlife rehabilitation specialist whom we volunteered for, Benson remained in the wild while I gave him twice-daily rounds of antibiotics and heapings of healthy meals. Benson figured out the routine after the second day. Each morning and each evening he would arrive and lie under the tree where his meals (with pills) were served, waiting patiently for me to deliver his goodies. One of the most endearing things he did during his recovery was to soak his paw in a tub of water, usually climbing into the tub and resting there, often falling asleep while I sat nearby. When he was done soaking, he allowed me to squirt a topical spray on his wound.

Gradually he was walking on all four legs again, and by the time he finished his medications, he had almost completely healed. Instead of begging for an easy meal, Benson resumed his independence, broadening his territory again, but returned every two to three weeks as if to let us know that he was okay.

I never saw Benson again after that fall. I would like to believe he found a territory to call his own.

**TRISH KIRK** WISCONSIN

# Bear Saves Human From Rattlesnake?

**12 NOON**: Our beautiful six-year-old sow "Knock" arrived as always with her three cubs. This is her second set of three! Two years ago she was a terrible mother and lost her cubs regularly but would always come to me (Kathy) for help. She would talk away to me and pull on my pants leg to go look for them. The cubs soon learned to come here when they couldn't find Mama and I would stand on the end of the deck calling her. It didn't take her long to respond and come up to reunite with the three. This year she is a very good mama and doesn't let them out of her sight.

1 p.m: After some quality time with this mama bear (me), Knock and cubs started to leave and headed over the rocks making their way toward the pond. As she went over the rocks she suddenly chuffed at something and sent her cubs up the nearest tree. She followed them up the same tree, remaining on the lower fork. I was in the process of going indoors but decided to investigate what was worrying her, thinking perhaps it was a large male bear or perhaps one of her two-year-olds who still hang around here. I walked toward the tree they were in, when she started to chuff and slap at the tree trunk. I could not see another bear so I walked closer, stepping up onto the rock to get a better view down the mountain and a view of the base of the tree they were

up. I was, at this stage, approximately 15 feet from the tree. From my view on the higher level, Knock was a little above eye level. As I stepped up onto the rock, I was speaking to her telling her I couldn't see another bear and it was okay, it was only me! She suddenly came down the back side of the tree and charged me. I must admit I DID get a fright but did not stop talking to her. The charge, which I expected to be a bluff, didn't turn out that way! She knocked me fairly gently with her shoulder, just enough to move me backwards. She then turned and slapped the ground. I looked down and there, not two feet from my feet was a timber rattler, approximately two feet long. I must be honest—I didn't stay around long enough to get a good look! I'm petrified of snakes (and cows)! All I know, it was partly coiled and partly on the move. I did not hear it! Once I moved away, Knock returned to her tree and back to her cubs. It is the first rattler I have seen in the 11 years we've been here, but other folks have seen them on the property.

For one hour Knock and her cubs remained in the tree and she continued to slap the tree and chat her teeth; the cubs seemed to be totally oblivious! One, in fact, just spread across a branch and slept. One tried to come down toward Knock but she sent him up higher. Stewart, who had been out, arrived home and I told him what was happening. He went out to investigate, but she vocalized at him as well, although she did not leave the tree.

2:30 p.m.: The snake must have left because she came down the tree, called her cubs down and spent about half an hour with us before wandering off.

Perhaps I'm crazy, but I like to think that this sow, whom we've known since she was 18 months, was protecting me like a faithful dog would do.

**KATHY HORNBY** WILDERNEST INN, ROUGH RUN, WV

# My First Day Living with Kodiak Bears

THIS IS MY FAVORITE BEAR STORY. Tales of giant bears like the Monarch of Dead Man Bay had drawn me to Kodiak Island before stepping into Bob Stanford's office. He said, "If you want to see lots of big brown bears and no people, I can drop you off at Karluk Lake where the red salmon are spawning right now. You'll have the lakeshore all to yourself, and for good reason!" Payment was made up front in cash and Bob shared his best bear stories as we flew over mountaintops already dusted with snow. We counted forty-three bears as he banked the floatplane for our landing. Unloading my provisions onto a bear trail was unavoidable here. Before taking off, Bob shoved a sawed-off twelve gauge into my hand. You might need this. Remember to put the red flag up if you have an emergency, or the white one if you need an early pickup. Someone might fly over and see your signal.

A cottonwood tree would provide some degree of shelter, so I relocated dry bags stuffed with camping gear, waterproof camera cases and a bear-resistant, 50-gallon barrel with the next month's supply of dried foods off the bear trail. The drizzle became a downpour before getting the tent set up, and my enthusiasm for a Kodiak adventure was dampened further upon realizing the cooking fuel was on its way back to town, stored in the float on Bob's side of the plane. Surrounded by bears, I had little choice but to go hungry or dine on kippered snacks and crackers, in the tent! When the storm finally lay down that night, the commotion of bears fishing along the lakeshore danced in my head. I was awakened before sunrise by a curious bruin running his nose along the tent wall, from my toes up to my nose. In those days before contemporary bear-safety practices, portable electric fences weren't used to establish a bear-resistant camp perimeter. (Even more frightening was a Montana grizzly sniffing through my bivy sack one night. At least in the tent, I felt not quite as vulnerable. But that's another story!) And satellite phones were simply unheard of. Otherwise, I'd have called Bob in the morning for the two gallons of white gas. As it was, with the cottonwood kindling soaked completely through, the joys of hydrating my dried goods in cold water for hours before dining became a necessary wilderness routine.

Cold oatmeal isn't that bad if you're hungry enough. However, it's not the taste that remains but the wonderment of bears splashing along the lake, occasionally coming up with salmon. Without exception, the bears focused on a survival mission and paid me no attention. Soon enough I regained confidence, packed my camera bag and slung the twelve gauge over my shoulder for some peace of mind. With more than a dozen bears in view, it didn't take long to wander upon a mother fishing in a deep pool with two spring cubs on the bank behind her. I tucked up along a tall clump of grass and set up my tripod to do what I'd come for. Like the others, she seemed oblivious, preoccupied with catching spawned-out salmon drifting through the slough. Her fascinating technique became the subject for my camera and I burned through film at an unsustainable rate. I was mesmerized by her uncanny filleting method, stripping the skin from head to tail and cracking the skull, then tossing the filleted salmon up to her cubs waiting on the bank. One cub seemed to get more than his fair share of the catch, and mother seemed to hurry her end of the process so the second cub could claim the next salmon without unwanted competition. The survival of both cubs seemed her priority.

I was looking down to change film when mother bolted from her fishing hole in a beeline, straight for me! In less than a heartbeat (or two), she stood towering over me on her hind legs, growling with her ears back and bashing her teeth for added emphasis. The twelve gauge lay at my feet, but I was frozen in fear. Her roar was so loud my torso resonated more violently than if standing in the front row at a rock concert. And her breath was nauseating, smelling like fish guts rotting in the sun, only much worse! Overwhelmed with trauma and in a state of psychological shock, it all seemed like an out-of-body experience. I had slouched involuntarily into a posture she may have correctly interpreted as submission. Still standing, her head was feet above mine. Then she dropped to all fours and perked her ears. Mother stared through and beyond me, her nose no more than a foot from my pounding heart. Then she woofed and gestured with her forepaw, like a traffic cop waiving cars into an intersection. With this command, a third cub darted from my blind side! She swatted it into the air with a blow that would have separated my head from its roost. It sent the cub plummeting into the slough, bawling as it swam to the opposite shore to attentive siblings.

Just as she had charged without warning, mother pivoted, tacitly returning to fishing as if all was well in her world again. Once the perceived threat to her third cub was resolved, she seemed to harbor no lingering hostilities toward the cub or this stranger at her fishing hole. Her point had been made clearly. Neither of us would need to learn this lesson again.

Two decades and countless close encounters later, I still revisit this Kodiak story. It often gives me pause to reflect on lessons for that next step into the bear's world and its psyche. On first hearing my story, some suggest wearing the twelve gauge on my shoulder would have allowed squeezing off a lifesaving round. But a heartbeat isn't much time. And in two or three, a hasty hip shot may have been fatal for both the bear and me. Others have proposed such intrusions into grizzly bear country are unwise and should be left to the experts. But all experts were once "as green as grass" and their paths are usually long and twisted. Had I been more attentive, I would have noticed the third cub and would have avoided the situation by moving away from the fishing hole. But as it was and without having to think about it, evolution had pre-wired me with fear, which can be a most beneficial emotion. Being too scared to run avoided a worst-case scenario in which mother would have likely attacked and mauled me, or worse. This is why experts advise never run, not only in an encounter, but when on grizzly ground where the unexpected unfolds step by careful step.

Scientific Footnote: Until recently, the Kodiak brown bear was considered a distinct subspecies of *Ursus arctos*. Modern DNA analysis shows the Kodiak populations to be distinct from grizzly bears of the northern Rocky Mountains but correlating highly with the brown bears living off the Alaska Peninsula. Outside scientific circles, it has become increasingly popular to refer to both of these bruin populations as Alaskan grizzly bears.

**BUCK WILDE** IDAHO

# Steps into the "Humanimal" Mind

**MEETING LYNN ROGERS** changed my view of grizzly bears and perhaps saved my life. A pioneering behavioral biologist, Lynn is to bears as Jane Goodall is to primates. Both are preeminent experts who live in the wild with free-roaming subjects. They've decided to study these wild animals in an open and approachable fashion where close encounters often become the norm. Sometimes it's difficult to say who's studying whom. Sitting beside a black bear or chimpanzee exposes these researchers to an element of risk, which they mitigate by communicating with body language that speaks louder than words.

Lynn is also a photographer with an interest in polar bears and grizzlies in addition to Minnesota black bears. He is famous for creating images from ground level taken from a prone position. I'd been a fan of his award-winning images but never dreamt we'd meet, until it happened unexpectedly one day in the wilderness of the Alaska Peninsula. The "last best place for bears" attracts photographers and filmmakers from around the world. I had been on the assignment of a lifetime for David Attenborough's BBC *The Life of Mammals* Series, but meeting Lynn Rogers made the more profound impression, reshaping my view of wildlife.

In responding to my question, "How can you lie in front of a polar bear or a grizzly without becoming lunch?" An upward gaze overcame Lynn for a moment, as he pondered before looking me in the eye. The bears are curious about us entering their world. They're also afraid of us, just like we're afraid of them. They are constantly weighing fear against their curiosity. I don't recall whatever else Lynn said. Here was this world-renowned biologist speaking of human-like emotions in wild animals, anthropomorphism, outright blasphemy to science!

His nugget of wisdom didn't fit my naïve view of wild minds. After all, I'd been charged by a dozen or so grizzlies and learned they were unpredictable and potentially dangerous. Mothers with cubs were especially troublesome. Something didn't line up, so my head began to ponder for another way of looking at Lynn's advice that might make more sense.

In the process of reading some academic articles about animal behavior, I began to notice references to *The Expression of the Emotions in Man and Animals* by Charles Darwin. Written shortly after *On the Origin of*

*Species, Expressions* was more problematic for the Victorian mind and has only recently been embraced by science. It's a pillar of behavioral biology. So I read it from cover to cover and appreciated Paul Ekman's editorial contributions too. (If you haven't noticed, he's the main character in *Lie to Me*, a show about the career of a body language expert contracted by government agencies and multinational corporations.)

Sure enough, Darwin's research has been confirmed; fear and curiosity are among the emotions shared across the animal kingdom. These are expressed via universal indicators that anyone can read as body language. This doesn't have to be rocket science. Every kid knows a dog with its ears back might bite. Since that first meeting with Lynn, I've learned to look at wild animals with a respect that some reserve only for humans, and I've also learned to be in touch with my intuitions, especially in detecting and assessing a potentially threatening situation. After stepping into the world of the wild psyche (that is the bear's and mine), not one grizzly has charged or otherwise seriously threatened me. Jane Goodall is surely familiar with Darwin's "other book" too, but Lynn Rogers' shared insights provided a budding wildlife photographer with a more solid paradigm for the "humanimal" mind.

This naturalist has been so fortunate to meet such icons as David Attenborough and Jane Goodall. But I must thank Lynn Rogers for starting my journey into the humanimal mind.

**BUCK WILDE** IDAHO

# Bird Seed À la Carte

**DURING THE SUMMER OF 2006**, I would put out bird feeders on a little cart I had. I had a small table standing in the cart and had different feeders on top of the table and hanging from it. I put the cart out during the hours that I was home and could keep an eye on it, and would bring everything in overnight or if a bear came around. However, I was also in the habit back then of scattering a lot of food on the ground for my birds to keep them coming around when the food cart was not out. The food on the ground is what the bear was after during the day, and, of course, it went for the food cart when that was out. I also had suet cages scattered out around my yard. Early on in the summer I left those suet cages out all day long until I realized the bear was going to be a regular in my yard; then I would only put them out when the food cart was out.

We had a fun summer with the bear that year. It was not a problem for us at all, and she and I developed an understanding of each other. As the summer progressed, she started to allow me to be outside with her, but we kept an imaginary boundary between us. As I moved around the yard, I would point in the direction I planned to go and would say, I'm going that way. She would side step to make room for me to move in that direction. If she was frightened or uncomfortable about something, she would go to the trees at the edge of the lawn and stand up against them. I can't tell you how many cars went by within a few feet of her where the drivers never saw her because she was hugging those trees. We had people drive up to the road in front of our house all of the time looking to see if the bear was there. I would go out and tell them what time they should come around to see her, because her timing was predictable. She and I learned to trust each other to the point that my husband was concerned. He felt I trusted her too much and should have been more cautious. She always came around in the morning before I left for work and in the evening when I got home. In the mornings I scattered the food on the ground and in the evenings I put the cart and suet cages out. She knew when to get here and always showed up at those times.

I never minded the bear eating the food off of the ground, but after that summer I discovered that the state of New Jersey has strict rules against feeding bears, so I had to change my ways. Now I put out my bird feeders during the summer months only when I'm here to watch them, and I rarely scatter any food on the ground. We still see bears, but they don't stick around like the one did that summer of 2006. I really enjoyed that summer with the bear and wish it could happen again, but I know it can't, so I relish the memories.

**MAUREEN LYNN** MONTAGUE, NJ

# Not So Tough After All

## FICTION:

If you see a black bear, it will likely attack.

## FACT:

Black bears almost never attack.

Truth be told, most bears run away from people. Bears that are used to seeing people may ignore them unless the people behave in unpredictable ways and cause the bears to run away. Since 1900, only 66 people have been killed by wild black bears in North America. To put that another way, only one black bear in a million kills someone and about one grizzly in fifty thousand kills someone. Comparatively, humans are far more dangerous, as 1 person in 18,000 murders someone in North America.

While very few bears are violent, their actions are often misunderstood. If a black bear doesn't flee immediately, it will sometimes stand up on its hind legs to get a better view of the situation. This can look intimidating, but it doesn't mean an attack is likely. Black bears also sometimes "bluff charge," but this is simply a display of fear and anxiety, and researchers from the North American Bear Center have seen hundreds of such charges. Not one led to an attack. What should you do if you see a black bear? Some recommend speaking calmly and backing away slowly, which is good advice because it minimizes the disturbance to the bear. But is that necessary for preventing an attack? No. In truth, people have reacted to bear encounters in about every way imaginable, and attacks are rare no matter what. But what if a person turned and ran? Would it trigger a predatory chase as some claim? No data substantiates that claim. In reality, we often hear, "I ran one way, and the bear ran the other."

# All I Wanted
# Was a Shower

**ALL I WANTED WAS A SHOWER.** We were camping in a little campground near Montreat, North Carolina, as part of a church-wide retreat when the fun began. The majority of the group were staying in the lodge about a half mile from the campground, but being the hardcore campers that we were, we chose to stay in the little campground just up the road. Our pop-up camper that had traveled from Cabot's Trail to Yellowstone was tucked neatly into the campsite not far from the bathhouse as we ventured back and forth from the lodge to be part of the group.

It was Saturday night and my wife and three daughters were enjoying the fellowship of the group at the lodge so I thought this would be a good time to hike back to the camper and get my shower in peace and quiet. Little did I know that my trip would be anything but peace and quiet!

I arrived at the camper in pitch dark since there was no electricity at the site and since we didn't want to leave lights on and run down our camper battery. I felt my way past my car and to the door of the camper and was relieved to make it inside and cut on the lights. As I readied my gear for the trip to the shower, I thought I heard something rustling outside the door. I carelessly threw open the door expecting to see maybe a raccoon, at the most. Nothing. I assumed the sound of the door opening must have frightened whatever it was away. As I went back to the task of emptying my pockets and gathering my shower paraphernalia, I again heard more rustling. This time being a little more cautious, I gently opened the door and shined the flashlight around the perimeter and saw nothing.

It hit me then that this was part of the problem! I realized that the trash can we normally placed by the door for paper and non-food trash was not turned over, as had happened many times over the years, thanks to squirrels, raccoons, and even skunks, but it was completely missing. At this point it hit me that the only critter that could carry away this trash can would not be a cute little raccoon that would pose for a photo for me, but rather a large critter that probably would not even be considered a critter at all!

It was at this time that the perceived need for a shower diminished quite a bit. I felt that my family probably needed my company at the lodge more than I needed a shower! I quickly gathered my belongings and decided to make a run for my car and drive the half mile to the lodge.

At this time, it may be helpful to understand the basic design of a pop-up camper. Once the top is raised, the beds on either end slide out with nothing below them but the support braces and the great outdoors. The only thing separating whatever is on the bed, such as people and . . . shower supplies . . . and whatever is beneath the bed, is about ⅝" of particle board and about 1½" of foam. This realization has since been burned into my consciousness.

Back to my escape. I opened the door very carefully, shining the flashlight everywhere I could from the safety of the little, flimsy camper door. Seeing nothing, I made a run for it. As I made it to the other side of a little table we always set up under the canopy and opened up the back hatch of the car to load my belongings, my courage returned somewhat and I turned to take a quick look at the camper door to convince myself that I was worried for no reason. Remember the ⅝" particle board and foam? Out from under this woefully inadequate barrier, directly below where I had stood arranging my toiletries, emerged a 10-foot-tall black bear (he was actually about 5'-6' tall, but at the time he might as well have been 10'!) I was approximately 15' away from him shining the flashlight in his face. Fortunately, I was just a few feet from my car door. Unfortunately, I had opened the back hatch where all the good smelling food was stored! Now all I could think about was that the bear would be enticed by the aromas coming from my car and that we might be sharing a ride back to the lodge. To close the hatch would mean walking towards the bear another seven to eight feet to reach the door.

I noticed the bear had averted his gaze from me to no doubt search for more delicacies around our camper, so I took my chance and quickly made it to the back of the car and closed the hatch. As I stood by the driver's door, ready for my escape, I once more shined the light in the direction of the bear. At this point he stood on his rear legs and our eyes locked for what seemed like an eternity. He then turned while still upright and looked into the windows of the camper placing both paws on the plastic just outside where I had been standing a few minutes earlier. Appearing content that there was no longer anything of interest in the camper, he went back down on all fours and lumbered into the darkness of the woods.

After making it back to the lodge and gathering a crowd around to explain how I fended off a vicious bear attack, my wife and our three girls joined me as we drove back to the campsite. The fact that they even agreed to spend the night in the camper with only that ⅝" particle board and a little canvas between us and the bear was nothing short of a miracle that one might expect on a church retreat. Upon arriving back at the campground, I cautiously surveyed the situation from the safety of the car and surmised that we were indeed alone. One by one we each made our way to the camper and were subsequently issued a metal pot and spoon with military precision by my wife. She then instructed us to keep these valuable weapons by our sides throughout the night to shatter the silence if any hint of our nocturnal visitor should return.

After settling in with our weapons by our side, courage welled up in me and I decided to take several flashlights (as if more light might deter an attack) and explore the perimeter of the campsite to hunt for evidence of my friend. One of my daughters did not want me to die alone so she joined me on my excursion. To my surprise, we actually found our trash can approximately 30 yards away in the woods complete with teeth marks from our visitor. We also discovered the probable attraction that instigated the initial visit: an empty sack that once contained half a bushel of freshly picked peaches that was inadvertently left on that little table under our canopy. Also left as souvenirs were a dozen or so peach pits beside the sack that were so clean that they looked as if they had cycled through a commercial dishwasher.

The next morning we awoke (actually we just got up; to awake would imply that some of us actually slept that night) to find no more evidence of our visitor. We packed up and left the campground after attending our church worship service, saying a few additional prayers of thanks that we survived the evening, and made our way home. To this day we keep the trash can as a reminder of our exciting evening, and pointing to the teeth marks as we tell our story around the campfire, the size and ferocity of the bear grow each time. By the way, I waited until we returned home for that shower!

**ROGER HOLLAND** SHELBY, NC

# Bear Sightings

MY FIRST ENCOUNTER with a black bear occurred on my first trip to the Boundary Waters Canoe Area in 1991. My best friend, his wife, three boy scouts and I were on day six of a ten-day trip. We pulled into a site on Lake Kekekabic in the late afternoon. Right before supper two people in a canoe came by and asked if we had seen any empty sites on the eastern end of the lake. They had set up camp just west of us and said when they checked out behind the site near the toilet, there were several bears feeding on a dead moose. We said there were no empty sites and I am not sure where they stayed. Around 6:00 after supper one of the scouts hollered, "Bear!" We had three tents set back about thirty yards from the fire and a lot of space between them. A very large bear walked from behind one of the tents and just stood there. It raised its head and looked around and sniffed the air for about thirty seconds. It then turned around and walked back into the woods and was not seen again. It is hard to describe the feeling you have in the wilderness being that close to a wild bear with nothing between you and it. Very exhilarating. It also made for a sleepless night.

The following year, six of us (all adults) made a return trip. Between the highway and Don Beland's lodge we crossed a small creek. A bear was foraging about twenty yards away from a creek bottom. We stopped and got out of the van (we did not approach the bear). It did not seem to mind us watching and slowly walked away down the creek, eating as it went. I believe now it was a yearling.

Our last trip to BWCA was in 1995. On the road to Two Harbors, about ten miles south of Ely, we saw a mother bear with three cubs cross the road in front of us. All these trips were in June. We went to the bear observatory at Anan Creek in Alaska in 1996. Here we saw four black bears fishing for salmon. No grizzlies. Later on during the trip we rented a car and drove from Skagway to Haines. To get there we drove 300 miles through a small portion of British Columbia and then to the Yukon. About thirty miles after crossing back into the United States, a grizzly mother with two cubs crossed the road in front of us. We stopped at a very respectful distance. After they had crossed, she stood up and looked at us (100 yards away) for about ten seconds, then ran into the woods.

**DAVE CAPPS** MT VERNON, IL

# Caught More than Salmon

**DURING ONE** of our annual salmon fishing trips to Alaska, we were on the Kenai River near Sterling when suddenly we spotted a bear in front of our boat. It was swimming across the river (we think it was a blackie) and it clamored up on shore at a full run straight through a camper's small tent. Apparently, the camper was sleeping inside as he came flying out wearing only his red long johns and waving a rifle. The look on his face was priceless and as he spun around in a circle; you could see him trying to figure out what had just happened. Of course, the bear was long gone. This was almost more fun than catching our King Salmon.

**ALOHA, GRACE HOSKINS NISHIGAYA** HONOLULU, HI

# Bear Story

I live on the Outer Banks of North Carolina and frequently visit the Alligator River National Wildlife Refuge to photograph black bears. The coastal area of North Carolina is the home of one of the densest populations of black bears in the world. In addition to the bears and many other critters, the refuge is the only place in the world where the endangered red wolf lives in the wild.

June and July is mating time for the black bears on the coast. During mating season, the males have only one interest. They do not eat for six weeks—they just seek out and mate with the females. One very early morning I was driving down the refuge road when I spotted a haggard male approaching the intersection. I stopped at the intersection and waited. The bear came within ten feet of the car, then turned towards a neighboring cornfield. He sniffed the wildlife-drive signpost, then lumbered off to a metal pole to mark his territory. Then he decided to come back to the sign, read it and mark it. He turned towards me and looked as if to ask "Do you really think wildlife are here?" Finally, off he went into the woods. He was on a mission and was no threat and had no interest in me. What a delightful way to start the day. It does not get any better than this.

I have had many wonderful experiences with the bears on this refuge. I do not approach, disturb or interact with the bears in any way. It is their home and I am a visitor there. I only enjoy their antics and take away great photos and very fond memories.

**JACKIE ORSULAK** OUTER BANKS OF NORTH CAROLINA

# Out of the Mouths of Babes

WHEN MY DAUGHTER WAS 3, we were on our way to Chisholm, Minnesota. We took Highway 210 until we hit Highway 169. It was summer, and we were on a long stretch of road surrounded by trees. We had not seen a car for a long time. In the distance, we saw something black on the road. It was just standing there. I slowed down as I got closer. It was a black bear. It just looked at us and we, it. Eventually, it walked off the road. My little girl, in her car seat in the back seat, was straining to watch the bear as it walked off the road. Her words after were priceless: "BIG ONE!"

**CINDY NELSON** FERGUS FALLS, MN

# Lost with the Bear

WE WERE IN JUNEAU in August of 2007. I was on a cruise to Alaska and we stopped in Juneau to visit the Mendenhall Glacier. We had been told by salespeople in Juneau that there were a lot of bears at the glacier and that people were going as soon as they got off work to try to see a bear. I was so excited about the bears (not so much about the glacier). When we arrived, I used the facilities and then I became separated from my group and was trying to find them when I came across a black bear. It looked smaller than I expected. Could it have been a yearling? I ran into a ranger who told me I needed to be with more people, so I found a group (not mine) and I followed them. We came across the bear again. It was across a small stream with salmon, and it tried to catch a fish but missed, then went on its way. I was thrilled to have seen it even though I wasn't with anyone to talk to about it. I was not afraid and the bear did run from us, which was good. I finally found my group and they had seen it too, but my husband missed the whole thing because he was looking for me. He was not happy, but he got over it!

**JOYCE NEIDLINGER** AURORA, CO

# Bear Chases the Dog

MY OLDEST SON, my mom, my sister, her daughter, and my brother Randy and his dog Smoky (a Mountain Cur, a good squirrel dog) went to the cabin for a summer outing. The cabin is a house my dad started renting as a hunting camp about 30 years ago. My mom had her pickup truck and after lunch we loaded up for a ride up the Big Hill. The Big Hill is pasture about a quarter way up the mountain filled with persimmon trees, cedars, red raspberries and coral berry. We got to the top and stopped to walk out an old road to look for red raspberries. My son stayed in the truck to listen to the radio. From there he could pick up rap stations from Raleigh, NC, about 140 miles away. Smoky went out ahead and dropped off the road on the downhill side. We had gone about 40 yards when we heard branches popping and something that sounded like a deer fawn the dog had surprised. The next thing you know the dog is back in the road running toward us with a bear right on its heels. Randy yells out, "Bear," and our crew starts scattering. My mom led the way and jumped up into the bed of the truck, not bad for an 80-year-old lady, and my sister and niece

**100**

weren't far behind. My brother and I were yelling, waving our arms and I was looking for a cedar to jump behind. The bear stopped about thirty yards from us, and we started whooping and I stepped back to high-five Randy when he yelled, "It's coming again." Again we waved our arms and it stopped about twenty yards away this time. We watched it run back, then went to the truck. Randy asked, "Did you see it?"

My niece said, "I saw the dog."

He responded, "If you saw the dog, you saw the bear; it was right on him." In hindsight, the sound we heard was a cub and the sow didn't want Smoky looking at it. Randy had told the story to a few people and added that Smoky was a good dog. He didn't chase the bear away; he brought it back for everyone to see.

DAVID JENKINS ROANOKE, VA

# The Occasional Bear

BEFORE WE WERE MARRIED, my husband bought a piece of property on the 11th Crow Wing Lake, outside of Akeley, Minnesota. He had been told that the bears' summer migration path was around the lake on their way to the Badoura State Forest.

When we were dating, he said that he had seen a bear once, maybe in 1991; it was in the driveway, and when he honked the truck's horn, it scampered away. In 1996, he was putting the finishing touches on a new deck, and heard a grunting sound beneath him. The deck is approximately 24 feet above ground, as the cabin is on a hillside. He peered between the boards and saw a bear, obviously perplexed as to the "roof" over its head where there had been none a day or two prior. Both my husband and the bear went on with their tasks, ignoring each other.

I didn't see a bear myself until this summer (2010). I saw it during the long, lingering summer twilight that only northern Minnesota has; it was a good-sized bear and ran very swiftly across the road in front of our truck. My husband estimated the bear at about 250 pounds and at least two to three years old. I haven't seen one again—wish I would. In the meantime, I thank them for taking good care of the cabin when we aren't there.

**ALEXIS TODD** PLYMOUTH, MN

# My Bear Afternoon

**WHILE ENJOYING AN EARLY FALL WALK** last year, I came across a scene right out of a Disney classic. As I slowly made my way up an old logging road, I noticed movement on the hillside above me. Balancing oh so carefully, a young bear was making his way down the length of a fallen tree. When he got to the end, he simply sat down to enjoy one of the last warm days of the season. With childlike wonder, he took in all that nature had to offer. He swatted at an insect that was buzzing around him, shaking his head vigorously. He toyed with the bloom of a late-summer wildflower, bouncing it back and forth on its long stem. His head turned from side to side, his nose in the air as he took in all of the sounds and smells that surrounded him: the serenade of a nearby chicka-dee, the chattering squirrels as they scurried around gathering their stash for the approaching winter. He cocked his head out of curiosity, not fear, at the bark of a distant dog. Eventually boredom won out, and he got down from his log and ambled off into the woods. I stood there and reflected on the last 10 or 15 minutes and what I had just witnessed. I will never forget the time that I shared with that young bear. He gave me a glimpse of the world through his eyes, eager to explore, ready for the next adventure that lay ahead. Yet, he took the time to slow down and savor a moment and to appreciate the beauty around him and what he already had within his reach. Perhaps a lesson for us all.

**SALLY BARR** CENTERVILLE, PA

# Let Sleeping Bears Lie

RAY, MY DAD, WAS AVID ABOUT NATURE and the outdoors and shared this legacy with his children and grandchildren. As an engineer, he was very precise about almost everything. We teased him about being able to tell the time of day by what he was doing. He enjoyed hunting and always carried a gun; but in his later years, he was really in the woods for the enjoyment of watching the activity of the northern Minnesota woods. His deer stand was ten miles north of Chisholm on Highway 73. However, when hunting, he would often find a different log to sit on while he enjoyed his 9 o'clock coffee and roll. On this particular morning, he told us, "I found a good stump to sit on. It was on top of this small hill so I had a good view of everything around me. I poured my coffee, got out my roll. The heat of the coffee felt really good because it was chilly that morning. As I was enjoying the scenery, I happened to look down between my feet. There were two eyes looking up at me. I looked a little closer, moving very little. It was then I realized I was sitting on top of a black bear's den. The bear must have smelled the coffee, opened his eyes, but decided he was too tired to join me. I very quietly put everything away and backed down the hill away from the bear. I hightailed it out of that area looking behind me to be sure I wasn't being followed. From that point on, I always took a little hike around any mounds to be sure I wouldn't sit on top of another den." When I was little and he told the story, I would always ask him if he was afraid. He'd respond, "Nah, black bears won't do anything to you especially when they're in hibernation. But it's always good to respect their nap and move away so you don't disturb them."

**RUTHANNE HYDUKE** IOWA CITY, IA

# Cat Chases Bear
# and Gets a Licking

I WATCHED AS A LARGE BLACK BEAR came into my yard and headed straight for my cat, Wely. Surprisingly, the cat sat calmly as the bear passed within 2 feet without a nod. As the bear disappeared into the woods on the other side of the yard, Wely ran after it. I yelled frantically. A half-hour later, the cat came home soaked with saliva from head to toe. I wish I could have seen the two of them together.

RITA GROSE ELY, MN

# Gus

THIS IS HOW IT ALL STARTED. On May 15, 2008, I was at my camp in north-central Pennsylvania. At 3:57 a.m. I heard a loud noise on my deck, and lo and behold, it was a black bear. As I tried to watch him through the window, he headed toward a trash can about twenty-five feet from my camper. He took the lid off and had himself a treat or two. I watched this bear for some time; then he turned and headed down through the campground, turning every trash can over he could until he was out of sight. I had been camping in this area for many years, mostly in a tent, so at this point I was happy I had upgraded to something with real walls. I was not afraid, just happy there was a wall between us at the time.

I love adventures, so the study of black bears began. I went to online sites and purchased books to find out everything I could about black bears and have been addicted ever since. As we all know, we were taught to fear them. I just had one problem—I had no fear of this bear. I would go out in the dark and sit at night listening for him to come down off the mountain, just to see if he would pick up my scent and know he could trust me as I would talk to him. By now I had given him a name—Gus. I was very careful not to get too close and let Gus decide that. He is just one amazing bear. He would come down off the mountain and allow me to get fairly close to him as I would talk to him. We have spent several years together, and I have always respected his mountain. I am a visitor in his world. Gus still comes to visit, but not as much as he used to. But when I least expect him, I look across the creek bed and there is Gus watching me. I have had a few other encounters with different bears but nothing like the trusting relationship I have had with Gus. Bears will always amaze us as we continue to let them teach us about their world.

**SUSAN YOST** WELLSBORO, PA

# Bear to the Rear

OUR FAMILY TOOK SUMMER CAMPING TRIPS to the national parks every year. Before our first trip to Yellowstone, Mom and Dad warned us that we might see bears in the campgrounds, and to be aware of them and not get too close. We pulled into the campground on our first evening, found a nice spot, and my older brother jumped out of the car to direct my dad into the space so we could set up our tents. As soon as he got set and started beckoning Dad to back up, Dad yelled, "Richard, there's a bear behind you!" Richard said, "Yeah sure, Dad, very funny." Then we all yelled, "There really is a bear behind you!" Richard rolled his eyes, and slowly turned around. You should have seen him scamper into the car when he saw we were not kidding. The bear slowly ambled away. It was our first up-close bear encounter. We've been back to Yellowstone many times and always see lots of bears.

**DONNA LAFFERTY REED** MESA, AZ

# A Brief Look at a Bear

I WAS VISITING ALASKA for the first time and had my camera on my lap ready to take a picture of any wildlife that I saw, and I especially wanted to see a bear. My husband was driving our motor home, and I thought I saw something dark a ways off the road and yelled, "Stop the motor home now!" He did and he backed up to where I saw this dark object. Well, it was a bear, and I did get to see it but I only saw its backside as it was walking away.

**CAROL PEARCE** ST PETERSBURG, FL

# Everyone Wants to See a Bear!

THE CARS IN THE LONG LINE AHEAD OF US came to a halt. I leaned out the Jeep's open window looking for the reason this time. We had not made much progress. The day was warm and sunny. It was so nice riding with the Jeep top off and having the summer wind blowing all around. But this long line of traffic prevented that. We were just crawling through the cove, and now we'd completely stopped! It was getting uncomfortably hot. "What kind of adventure is this?" my husband restlessly said. Well, the cove was beautiful. There was a small herd of horses grazing peacefully in the distant pasture. Beyond them rose the gentle mountains of Cades Cove, Tennessee. If the cars would just start moving again, the one-way road was tree-lined ahead. At least we could look forward to a little shade. I got out my binoculars and started to focus on an interesting shape in the middle of the field. "We could have avoided all this if we had just hiked!" suggested my hubby. Unfortunately, he had mentioned this earlier. I had dragged my feet, choosing a leisurely morning, and so now it was way too hot to hike. Besides, I told him, it would be too scary to hike in the cove. I had heard there were bears there. Bears in the cove, bears in the woods, and this long line of cars! Cars of people in search of bears! We had taken a hike the previous day with a park ranger, and even she had talked about bears. Everyone wanted to see a bear. All that my hubby and I wanted was to enjoy the beauty of the cove. After what seemed like eternity, the cars started to move. Relief! A gentle breeze cooled our faces. But within five minutes, an abrupt stop. Two guys in a car ahead jumped out of their car like they were running to a fire. They jumped the fence like lions after prey. One held a camcorder. The other yelled excitedly. In the field, two little black bear cubs scampered quickly as two bear-crazed guys chased them. All I could honestly think was that those guys were going to run right into mama bear. And we were sure to be witnesses to their gruesome deaths.

I have always had an attachment to bears. They are furry and cute, but even so, I was always afraid of the thought of encountering a real bear in the woods. The day at Cades Cove surprised me. The cubs ran into the woods and climbed a tree. No mama ever came out to eat the cub chasers like I thought would happen. In fact, the next day, we decided to be brave, and hiked in Cades Cove, with the bears. I was, quite honestly, terrified. We armed ourselves with bear bells and my hubby assured me we'd be OK. And we were. We had a wonderful time and even got to see another bear, sitting in a field, in the far distance, eating away. You could only see the top of her head and two adorable black ears sticking up above the tall grasses.

**CINDY TERRY** WEST LIBERTY, OH

# He Liked Me

**ABOUT 10 YEARS AGO** my husband and I were snowmobiling in Conover, Wisconsin. We came around a corner and found a group of snowmobiles, and their riders standing off to the side. I was afraid there had been an accident, but someone came up to us and said there was a bear in the trail. My jaw dropped; I was shocked! Being an avid bear lover, I was frozen with excitement and didn't know what to do. Someone said, "Oh, you can walk up to him; he won't hurt you." I could see my husband saying something but his words seemed to fall on deaf ears. I slowly approached the bear and sure enough, the little guy was quite sleepy on that warm early March morning. I was able to give him a little pet on the head! As I was doing that, my husband was turning our snowmobiles around in the opposite direction, thinking a mama bear had to be lurking somewhere. I was shocked almost to the point of being in tears I was so happy! We hung around as long as possible (me right up front, my hubby way in back) and waited until the bear just walked off by himself. I'll admit, it probably isn't a good idea to walk up to a wild animal, *but it was one of the most exciting moments in my life!* I'll never forget it, ever, and that experience fueled a passion for bears that had been there long before this encounter. I have the utmost respect for bears and look forward to more encounters like this, in the beautiful Wisconsin north woods!

**CORRINA SMET** KAUKAUNA, WI

# I Told You You'd See a Bear

**ON OUR AUGUST 2009 VACATION**, my husband Jeff and I visited Yellowstone Park. I was hoping to see a bear or two. Jeff kept saying, "Oh, you'll see a bear; we will be in bear country." Well, we saw a moose, an eagle, buffaloes, etc., inside the park but no bears. After leaving Yellowstone Park, we hadn't traveled more than a mile when the car in front of us stopped suddenly. The man's camera was hanging out of his car. We looked to his left and there it was—a grizzly bear! Jeff was so excited he couldn't remember how to operate the camcorder, so I reached for my camera. Then the bear started walking towards us. He walked right up to the window and stared right at us. I think he was hungry and thought the camera was food. When he realized we were not going to feed him, he went to the car behind us. How exciting it was that I saw a bear after all. Jeff looked at me and said, "See, I told you, you'll see a bear."

**DEBRA TRACEY** PEARLAND, TX

# Before I Learned Better

**I HAVE HAD MANY BEAR ENCOUNTERS** in my outdoor adventures. I used to be afraid of bears, but they intrigued me at the same time. At that time, I was an avid mountain biker, and my daily ride with my dog Black Jack took me along an old railroad bed that runs adjacent to the Lehigh River in Jim Thorpe, Pennsylvania. One particularly hot and humid day, I decided to leave Black Jack at home. Halfway down to the next town, a bear ran out of the woods and crossed right in front of me to get to the river. My heart was pounding so hard, and I think my legs grew stronger because I found myself in the next town quickly. I even warned a runner on the trail about the bear. Of course, my fear took me up the mountain to my sister's house as I refused to bike back up to my house. My sister loaded my bike and took me home. My husband just laughed and said, "They are there all the time, Suzi . . . what is wrong with you?" It was a long time before I traveled that stretch again. How ignorant was I?

**SUZI OWENS** TIOGA, PA

# Meeting Mama Bear

I **CHERISH THE WONDERFUL MEMORIES** of the summers I spent in Ely at my grandmother's cabin on a lake. On one hot summer afternoon, probably in July, my 12-year-old cousin and I (age 10) wandered down the trail, and we went deeper into the woods than we were supposed to. We were just exploring, kicking rocks, being kids with nothing to do. We both saw the cub at the same time and froze in astonishment. The cutest little bear was about 20 feet ahead of us on the side of the trail. We crept a little closer, trying not to make any noise. All of a sudden, mama bear came from behind a big rock and stopped. To us she looked HUGE, especially compared to the cub. Mama bear huffed at us but did not make a move. We, on the other hand, hightailed it as fast as we could run back to the cabin. We were covered with scratches from the brush, and stickers were all over our pants and socks. My cousin and I did not speak of the incident, fearing we'd get in big trouble. We stayed in the cabin the rest of the day, peering out the window to make sure mama bear had not followed us. All these many years later, the experience of seeing the bears remains a vivid one, and it always brings a smile to my face.

**JACKI CROFT TAYLOR** DESTIN, FL

# Resisting Phobia

BY VIRTUE OF LIVING in Wisconsin's beautiful north woods for over 31 years, I have had numerous black bear encounters. I also have several videos of the black bears visiting our home, sitting on our front entryway, and in general making themselves comfortable. One year in late spring, my husband Ron invited me to go with him deep into the woods surrounding our home. It was time to stretch our legs after a long winter of cabin fever. Little did we know that this innocent hike would end with a bear encounter.

We were nearing the end of our hike when we emerged from the woods and onto a gravel road. At the exact moment that our feet hit the gravel, so did a black bear's. It wasn't ten feet from us. She was a relatively small bear at about 225 lbs. What was odd was that she exited the woods on the same side of the road as we did. How did she not wind us? There was a slight breeze that day, perhaps in our favor.

This black bear encounter was surreal, as we scared each other half to death! It took both parties a full five seconds of staring to realize that we should go our separate ways. I should say that the bear and I understood that concept, but apparently my husband did not receive that memo, as he turned right around and followed the bear back into the woods. I was not sure what his motive was at the time, and I was not about to follow him to find out. I was already walking briskly backwards in the direction of our home, never taking my eyes off of the bear.

Later when Ron returned safely home, he told me that curiosity had gotten the best of him and he wanted to know if there were any cubs following her and also if she had a bed nearby. I, on the other hand, have a phobia of bears and truly do not understand why. I can name seven face-to-face encounters that I have had with the black bears near my home; in each episode the bears appeared more frightened of me than I was of them. They certainly do not stay around long after they have seen you or smelled you. After 31 years of living in the bear's habitat and knowing full well that they are more afraid of us than we are of them, I should be getting more comfortable around them, but instead, this phobia is getting worse. This is the first year that I have carried pepper spray with me when taking my walks along our gravel road. This is also the first year that I have ceased working my compost pile as it has suddenly dawned on my that I am inadvertently feeding the bears. When I add kitchen scraps to the compost bin, the bears visit for their easy meal. Watching Lily and Hope this past winter and now spring, summer and fall of 2010 has been a blessing as maybe it will help me be more accepting and understanding of the bears that live among us.

**GEORGIANN O'BRYAN** BRUCE, WI

# Got Milk?

**ABOUT EIGHT YEARS AGO**, we owned a llama breeding farm. Many beautiful babies were born there to some delighted moms. One especially lovely little cria didn't seem to be gaining weight as he should, and on the second day we found that mom had mastitis. Out came the baby bottles and a couple of days of feeble feedings. The next afternoon, I got a hold of the squirmy little fellow and began attempting to get him to drink. A nearby stud had been pacing on my arrival, which was very unusual, and as I began working at getting the nipple between the little guy's gums, the stud began actually alarm calling. I looked around for the usual danger and saw nothing. Suddenly the little guy figured things out and started wolfing down the much-needed milk. The stud continued alarming. As I shifted positions and baby got comfortable, I happened to look up into the tree that we stood beneath. There, peering down at us, not 10 feet above, was a black bear. No wonder there was such a commotion. I looked at the guzzling cria, then back at the bear. My heart started to pound a little and thoughts of being jumped on and eaten did cross my mind (although now I know that this was not likely). Nevertheless, I made what I considered both a defiant and brave decision, based on my knowledge of bears at the time. I looked up and said, "This baby is going to finish his bottle and then, I am going to run!" Both happened. Junior finished his bottle for the first time, and I grabbed him and ran, dropping him beside his mother as I flew past her. From the safety of the house, I watched the bruin, who was not really very large at all, climb down the tree and amble towards the creek. Teddy, the stud, settled down, and Junior began gaining weight and was back to enjoying fresh milk from mom within a week.

**ROSEMARY BELCHER** HUDSON'S HOPE, BC

# Enough Room
# for All of Us

IT WAS A COOL EARLY-MAY MORNING, and I was out hiking through my wooded property west of Ely, Minnesota. I always knew that bears lived and foraged in the area, but I had only caught glimpses of these beautiful animals. That all changed soon enough—a huge black bear was coming down the trail right towards me and it was followed by two little fuzzballs trying to keep up. I stopped and stood totally still, not moving a muscle. The bear was just as surprised to see me as I was her. She stood up on her two back legs and started to sniff the air. After what seemed liked hours (but was only seconds) she got back on all fours and just stood there, looking at me as if saying, "We're not turning around, so you'd better." I took this as a cue to back up slowly and walk away. I surely thought the bear could hear my heart thumping as I moved away. It allowed me to leave safely, and I thanked mama bear for letting that happen. I saw her two more times that summer, and both times, she saw me; we looked at each other and then moved on. We gave each other plenty of room to do our own thing that day in the woods. I have so much respect for these magnificent animals, and I know that they respect humans as well. I share my woods with all creatures and I think we can enjoy each other's company as long as we just look and never touch.

**STEVE HERRICK** ELY, MN

# Bear Encounter!

IN JULY OF 1990, my husband Tim and I took a trip out west in our Jeep to visit sites in Montana and South Dakota. Our destination was Yellowstone National Park. The night we arrived at the east entrance to the park we were too late to get a reservation to camp. We were told that in the morning there were always sites available, and we should camp in the Shoshone National Forest and come back early the next morning. We pitched our tent there in Shoshone and spent the night. Next morning, just as the sun was coming up, we left everything there and drove to the campsite that allowed tent camping and made our reservations. Once done, we started driving back to our camp site in the National Forest to pack up and come back. We were about a mile from the East entrance to Yellowstone, still in Yellowstone, when we saw cars pulled over to the side of the road. We knew this meant something of interest was there, so we pulled over as well. The Shoshone River is next to the road, and it was also near our campsite in the National Forest. Across the river, on the bank, was what we had come to Yellowstone to see: a bear! At first glance she was hidden in the trees on the far side of the river. She was watching us as we were watching her. She eventually started to go along the river on her way . . . followed by her two small cubs! Once we got a good view of her, we could see the telltale hump on her shoulders that told us this was a grizzly mama bear. As great as it was to see her, I was, of course, afraid she would be annoyed with us there with her cubs. The only safe place for us to take refuge in should she cross that very shallow part of the river was in our Jeep . . . our soft-top Jeep! I told my husband that if she crossed the river, I was going into someone else's car. Of course, she didn't cross the river and just kept walking with her cubs looking for food. The cubs stayed behind their mother and even played with each other as they passed us. What an experience.

We also travel to the Smoky Mountains every spring. In the spring of 2010 we had to cross the Smokies to get to the Biltmore Estate due to a road closure. On our way back we actually had a chance to see two mama bears with their single yearling cubs, one set near Laurel Canyon. I have gone to the same place for six or seven years, and this was my first time to see any black bears. I'm glad that we had to do the roundabout way so we had the chance to see these gentle giants.

**BARBARA LOZIER** LIBERTY TOWNSHIP, OH

# A Shared Encounter

WHEN I MARRIED MY WIFE TERI seventeen years ago, I was excited to become part of her rich lifelong cabin heritage. My wife grew up in a family that owned a small cabin in the woods of northwestern Wisconsin. Appropriately enough, it was located on Big Bear Lake. We enjoy going there often and we spend as much time with our family, children and friends there as we can. The area has a nice variety of wildlife, and we often get to enjoy sightings of whitetail deer, grouse, turkey, owls, hawks, merlins, loons, fox, eagles, and yes, sometimes even black bear. Over the years we have had bears come into the yard on several occasions seeking bird feeders and checking out the grills and garbage cans for possible treats. The infrequent sightings and stories of sightings by neighbors only fueled my imagination and desire to see more.

On a morning several summers ago, I was alone on the upper St. Croix River canoeing and fly fishing for smallmouth bass. I had been on the water for nearly an hour and had just quietly maneuvered my canoe into a spot near a section of bank that looked like promising fish-holding cover. As I began to strip line out of the fly reel with my eyes focused on the water, I heard a tremendous commotion from on the bank. It was a sound like I had never heard before and it lasted only seconds. Soon my eyes were drawn to the source . . . a black bear was climbing and scratching its way hurriedly down from a nearby tree only to melt away deep into the forest, no doubt disturbed from its midday slumber by my sudden arrival and the clacking of my reel.

In the spring and early summer of 2010 I heard that neighbors had spotted numerous bears up at the cabin and there were even tales of one very large bear in the area. My excitement level was rising and I was filled with hope to see yet another bear, perhaps the big bear. One weekend my lifelong friend and fellow outdoor enthusiast Dave was to spend the weekend with us at the cabin. Dave is a wildlife photographer and loves to wander the cabin area in search of subjects for his hobby. Of course, when he arrived, I promptly filled his head with all the stories of recent bear sightings just to mess with him a bit. I knew this made him a bit uneasy. In the mornings Dave typically wakes up early and walks up the driveway with his camera gear in search of photo opportunities and the next morning was no different. I awoke to find he had already left the cabin, so I started out down the same path to find him. Along a curve in the driveway, down by the swamp, I saw him up ahead of me, but he did not see me. So I quickly closed to within 40 yards of him and then took cover behind a small pine tree and began to shake it violently while growling my best bear imitation. The startled look on his face was priceless. I revealed myself and walked up to him feeling like my mission had been accomplished when all of a sudden I heard it again . . . that unmistakable sound I had heard only one other time—that day back on the river. I immediately shouted, "BEAR!" and we ran back near where I had hidden behind the pine tree. Sure enough, it was a bear coming down from a giant pine tree; but not just one bear—there were two, a sow with a yearling cub. Little did I know that the whole time I was pretending to be a bear to scare my friend, we were being watched by real bears high in their morning perch. We were now only 35 yards from them, and I could hear the sow making nervous sounds with her mouth. She stayed at the base of the big pine and kept the yearling up in the tree. At one point the yearling tried to come down, and she nudged it in the hindquarter with a loud woof that sent the cub scurrying back up to the first set of branches where it settled in and eventually began napping. We were able to enjoy them and photograph them from this position for nearly an hour before they finally climbed down and melted silently into the swamp.

**JACK RIEDEL** SHOREVIEW, MN

# Mothers
# and Cubs

# FICTION:

Black bears are very defensive of their cubs.

# FACT:

Black bears rarely attack in defense of their cubs.

The old saying "Never get between a mother and cubs" is often wrongly generalized to all bears. It's actually a warning about grizzly bears, as 70 percent of killings by grizzly bears occur when mothers defend their cubs. In comparison, since 1900, only one of the 66 killings involving black bears appeared to be in defense of cubs. Non-fatal attacks by black bear mothers are also rare; we know of only six such attacks in the last century.

In fact, when bear biologists in Ely routinely captured and held screaming black bear cubs, the mothers commonly bluff-charged, but they typically turned and retreated at about 20 feet. None have made contact.

# Snuggling Four Cubs

ONE OF MY MOST MOVING EXPERIENCES with black bears was a visit to a den with my husband Lynn on March 18, 1984. After snowmobiling miles through beautiful winter scenery, we tranquilized the bear so we could change her radio collar. Soft noises came from the den. Cubs! Lynn reached under the tranquilized mother and gently lifted out not two or three but four cubs and tucked them inside my wool jacket. One male and three squirmy females dug their little claws into my wool sweater and snuggled to me. I'll never forget seeing them close their eyes and relax as I stroked their little heads and paws. A few minutes later, while Lynn was changing the radio collar on the mother, the cubs quietly crawled up onto my neck and shoulders and took one of their first looks at the world. When Lynn came to weigh them, they dug their claws into my sweater as if they didn't want to leave. Lynn gently loosened their Velcro grips and looped a soft cord under the armpits of each. One by one, he lifted them with a small scale. Each swung quietly in an upright position, looking around as Lynn read their weights. We could see their furry tummies. After Lynn returned the waking mother to her den, it was my privilege to snuggle those precious bundles into her deep fur. A month later, she led the cubs out of the den and her radio collar began revealing habitats she used for food and safety. Being able to hold the cubs and be part of discoveries that can help them are memories I will always cherish.

**DONNA ROGERS** ELY, MN

# Bear in the Batter

ANVIL LAKE, in Northern Wisconsin's Nicolet National Forest, was a summer utopia for two young city girls from Milwaukee. It was full of trees, lakes, deer, trails, swimming, camping, hiking. My cousin Pat and I were those two girls, excitedly staring out the car window as the scenery changed to Up North vistas and roads became narrow, sun-dappled paths under arching trees. When my family's car arrived at Anvil Lake Campground, we were delighted to discover that our favorite site was available. Jumping out of the car, we all pitched in to unpack and erect the tent that would be home for me, my brother, my mother and father, Pat, and our miniature dachshund Jolie. We tied her to the base of a tall pine where she could watch as we worked.

In a short while, Jolie interrupted our work with frantic barking. Despite commanding her to be quiet, she continued to bark and pull on her rope, sometimes turning to jump on the tree's trunk. Ceasing our chores, we went over to untie her, intending to put her in the car to curb her noise ... until we looked up the tree. Imagine our shock at seeing two black bear cubs high in the pine!

We didn't know whether to be frightened or fascinated. Where was the mother bear? Would she arrive to rescue the cubs and threaten us? Oh, but the cubs were so cute! We had never seen real bears in the wild. This was an adventure!

But the wisdom of adults prevailed. My parents had intended to go out to eat that evening, leaving us at the site. Instead, they loaded all of us into the car and took everyone to dinner. Our hope was that the cubs would leave of their own accord, and that was what happened. When we returned, they were gone. Assured that the cubs had disappeared, we went to bed. Jolie, our early warning system, was snuggled in my sleeping bag.

The next morning, we awoke to a delightfully funny sight. The family camping next to us had apparently left their site after a pancake breakfast, but they had not bothered to wash their breakfast dishes or put away the remaining milk or pancake batter. Two small black and hungry visitors had showed up. Climbing onto the table was no problem, and we caught them using their little tongues to lick the plates. Apparently still eager for more, they knocked over the bowl of pancake batter and a carton of milk. Milk ran over the table and onto the ground. One cub crawled under the table to lick the liquid on the ground. Batter dripped onto the youngster's head and as both lapped up milk and batter, their heads and muzzles became covered in splotches. The sight was so funny and charming that we could only laugh. It really looked like something out of Disney!

For the remainder of our stay, my cousin and I kept looking for signs of the babies while exploring trails near the campground. We never saw them again, but we did see a ranger who told us that the cubs were probably orphaned and that if they remained in the campground near humans, they would have to be captured and moved to a new home far from Anvil Lake. When we finally left Anvil Lake, we wished the cubs well, hoping they would learn to be adult wild bears in their own environment.

**KATHY HERMANN AND PAT BRAASCH**
STEVENS POINT, WI AND REYNOLDSBURG, OH

Printed in the USA
CPSIA information can be obtained
at www.ICGtesting.com
JSHW060755140424
61126JS00006B/17

9 781591 933847